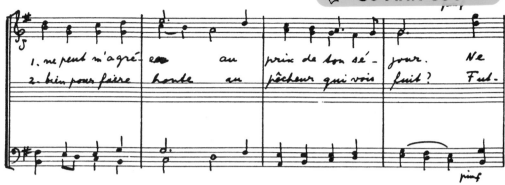

1. ne peut m'agré- ea   au   prix de ton sé- jour.   Ne
2. bien pour faire honte   au   pêcheur qui vois fuit?   Fut-

Detroit Studies in Music Bibliography, No. 71

Editors
J. Bunker and Marilyn S. Clark
University of Kansas

Henk Badings, 1907-87

by *Paul T. Klemme*

Harmonie Park Press   Michigan

Catalog of Works

Endsheets:
'Trois Romances' pour choeur masculin, 1950:
   (*Front*): a. O Nuit, heureuse Nuit (pages 7 and 8)
   (*Back*): b. Gai Rossignol Sauvage (pages 9 and 10)
Score reprinted with the permission of Donemus
Paulus Potterstraat 16
1071 CZ AMSTERDAM
The Netherlands

Frontispiece:
Henk Badings on the occasion of his 80th birthday, 1987

Published by
Harmonie Park Press
23630 Pinewood
Warren, Michigan 48091

Editors, J. Bunker Clark
Book Design, Elaine J. Gorzelski
Typographer, Colleen McRorie

Library of Congress Cataloging in Publication Data

Klemme, Paul, 1957-
     Henk Badings, 1907-87 : catalog of works / Paul Klemme.
          p.   cm. -- (Detroit studies in music bibliography ; no. 71)
     Discography: p.
     Includes bibliographical references and index.
     ISBN 0-89990-065-8
     1. Badings, Henk, 1907-   --Thematic catalogs.   I. Title.
II. Series.
ML134.B157A2 1993
016.78'092--dc20   93-31384

CONTENTS

PREFACE

Henk Badings occupies a position as one of the most important Dutch composers of the twentieth century. His numerous works are supported by writings on music and many years of teaching and guest lecturing at schools of music around the world. It is hoped this catalog will serve as a useful resource for composers, musicologists, performers and music lovers seeking information about the compositional output of this distinguished Dutch composer.

The catalog includes:

1. A brief biography.

2. A list of abbreviations.

3. A directory of Badings's publishers with their addresses and identifying abbreviation.

4. A complete list of works including arrangements of folksongs. The list of works has been classified by genre and is arranged alphabetically within each category. Each entry is given a "W" number and provides information such as date of composition, publisher, duration, medium of performance, notation of original language, literary source, a translation of all non-English titles and movements, sequence of movements and, when available, the commission for the work, its dedication, and the date of the premiere performance.

5. A discography of commercially-produced sound recordings, arranged alphabetically by title. Catalog number, performers, date of composition are listed. When available, album title and contents are included. Each entry is given a "D" number.

6. A list of articles written by Badings on music grouped according to language and arranged in chronological order.

7. An annotated bibliography of writings about Badings and his music. Each entry is given a "B" number.

8. Four appendices, of which Appendix 1 is a cross-referenced list of educational music and Appendix 2 is a cross-referenced list of music intended for youth and amateur orchestra. Appendix 3 is an alphabetical list of compositions, including cross-referenced subtitles and working titles along with performing forces. Appendix 4 provides a chronological list of Badings's compositions including subtitles and performing forces.

9. A complete index of names, titles, and selected subjects.

ACKNOWLEDGMENTS

I am indebted to Mrs. Henk Badings for the countless hours that she spent in proofreading and assisting with translations. I wish to thank Pieter van Moergastel, professor of music at the Brabants Conservatorium, Tilburg, Netherlands for his generous assistance and early work on the choral compositions. Also, I wish to acknowledge Leo Samama for his assistance with detailed biographical information and some careful proofreading. I am grateful to Dr. William Brandt, professor emeritus, Washington State University, for proofreading and advice on outlay of the catalog. My thanks to the staff at the Humanities Research Center, Washington State University, for their help. Finally, I am indebted to Washington State University for financial support of this project through summer stipend grants.

BIOGRAPHY

Henk Badings was born of Dutch parents at Bandung, Indonesia, on 17 January 1907. After his parents' sudden death in 1915 he was sent to the Netherlands in the care of a guardian who forbade him to pursue a career in music. He therefore enrolled as a student in mine geology and engineering at Delft Technical University. He graduated *cum laude* in 1931 and subsequently became a lecturer in the department of geology at the same university.

Badings was self-taught as a composer. In 1930, while still studying at the Technical University, he wrote a symphony which was performed by the Concertgebouw Orchestra of Amsterdam. As a result his name was quickly brought before the public and press. Two years later he wrote the Second Symphony and dedicated it to Eduard van Beinum, who conducted the première with the Concertgebouw Orchestra and performed it several times on the orchestra's first tour of the United States.

Following several years of geological research, which involved extended tours in Europe, Badings became a full-time professional musician. He was appointed Lecturer in Composition and Theory in 1934 at the Holthaus Conservatory in Rotterdam and became co-director of the Amsterdam Music Lyceum in 1937. In 1941-45 he directed the State Music Conservatory in The Hague. During the next decade and a half he became a free-lance composer; he organized an electronic studio for Philips in 1956, which was moved to the University of Utrecht in 1960. He was appointed Professor of Acoustics and Information Theory at the same institution in 1961-77. Badings held the position of Professor of Composition at the Staatliche Hochschule für Musik in Stuttgart, Germany, in 1962-72, and simultaneously was invited for guest lectureships at the University of Adelaide, Australia, and Point Park College, Pittsburgh, U.S.

Badings's international reputation was first established by his orchestral works, especially by his Third Symphony, Symphonic Variations, and his first Double Concerto for Two Violins and Orchestra. His complete works, however, span the spectrum of vocal and instrumental music in both small and large forms. His catalog of compositions consists of 15 symphonies, 50 other orchestral works, 48 concertos, 3 oratorios, 9 cantatas, 10 works for chamber orchestra, and 140 chamber music pieces ranging from solo sonatas and educational compositions to sextets and an octet. Badings's output also includes 6 operas, 10 ballets, 26 organ works, 31 compositions for the 31-tone temperament, 10 carillon pieces, 60 incidental works for stage and theater, 10 compositions for film, 26 electronic music settings, and 255 accompanied and unaccompanied choral works for all kinds of ensembles including female, male, mixed, and children's chorus. He has also written 75 essays on music theory.

From the start of his career Badings was preoccupied with problems of tuning and tonality. As early as 1924, he first used an octatonic tonality in which the scale consists of alternate tones and semitones. Later, he worked out a system of harmony based on a relationship between the overtone series and the undertone series as applied to equal temperament. In attempting to approach his ideal tuning more closely he began using microintervals. He built a 31-tone siren in 1945 and his first 31-tone composition appeared in 1952. Examples of his 31-tone works include five sonatas for two violins, 1963-84, and smaller pieces for a specially constructed organ in Haarlem. Badings further extended his range by incorporating concrete and electronic sounds into his works. A number of purely electronic works emerged, as well as compositions combining concrete and electronic sound-sources with traditional instrumental and vocal sound. He composed six such scores for the ballet, some of which were performed in opera houses such as the Wiener Staatsoper. In the same category is the incidental music for stage and cinema and two radiophonic operas. *Orestes*, which won the Prix Italia in 1954, was broadcast by the BBC in an English translation and by the Bayerischer Rundfunk in German. The English version was later broadcast all over the world by 900 radio stations. Electronic sound was also used in the dream scene of Badings's opera *Martin Korda D. P.*, the opening work of the Holland Festival of 1960. Another notable use of electronic sound is in Badings's chamber opera *Salto mortale*, which gained distinction in the Salzburg Opera Competition of 1959. In this work the entire accompaniment is electronic, making it the first such opera ever conceived. In 1956 Badings was invited to build an electronic studio at the Philips Research Laboratory in Eindhoven.

In 1959 Badings's research took him yet further, this time into the use of the computer for musical analysis and composition. His Toccata 1 and Toccata 2 are based upon a computer generated tone-series. His use of the computer in investigating the psychology of music, and the logic of musical composition, was also very fruitful. His discovery of the relationship of tempo to the probability-rate of tone-duration was published in his article "Over tempo en toonduur"

(1977). He further developed a method of dating the several melodic lines in motets by Machaut based on the probabilities of tone-qualities. In research into the piano works by Haydn, he developed methods of dating by means of probabilities of tone-qualities and harmonic relationships.

Despite his work in electronic and computer composition, most of the more than 600 compositions of Badings are mainly for traditional resources: orchestral music, choral works, and chamber music. His compositions have won many prizes, including the Netherlands Prize, 1935 (String Quartet 1); Prize of the Dutch Government, 1950 (Symphony 5); Radio Nederland Prize, Hilversum, 1950 (Symphonic Variations 1); Radio Diffusion Française, Paris, 1951 (*Java en poèmes* for mixed unaccompanied choir, and *Trois Ballades* for unaccompanied female choir); Jef Denijn Prize, Malines, 1951 (Suite 2 for carillon); Academia Chigiani Prize, Siena, Italy, 1952 (Quintet 5); first and second Paganini Prize, Genoa, 1953 (Sonatas 2 and 3 for solo violin); Malines, Belgium, 1954 (Suite 3 for carillon); Prix Italia, 1954 (*Orestes*); Dutch Government Prize, 1955 (Overture 5); Salzburg Award, 1959 (*Salto mortale*); Premio Marzoto Prize, Venice, 1964 (Double Concerto 1 for Two Pianos); Prize of the Australian Film Festival, 1965 (*Sound and Image*); Prix Italia, 1971 (Cantata 7).

Almost every composition by Badings was commissioned. Notable examples of these include an orchestral work for the centenary observance of the Vienna Philharmonic Orchestra (*Symphonic Prologue*, 1939), a symphony for the 50th anniversary of the Concertgebouw Orchestra (Symphony 5, 1949) and, for the Holland Festival, Symphony 6, 1953, and an opera, *Martin Korda D. P.*, 1960. He also composed a symphony for the Louisville Symphony Orchestra (Symphony 7, 1954), an orchestral work for the North German Radio (Symphony 8, 1956), an opera for the South African Radio (*Asterion*, 1957), an overture for the Cork Festival (*Irish Overture*, 1961), and a triple concerto for the commemoration of the 750th anniversary of Eindhoven (Triple Concerto 3, 1981).

Many honors and awards were bestowed on Henk Badings during his career. In 1939, the Hanseatic Foundation of Hamburg awarded him the Rembrandt Prize, and the Unesco Rostrum of Composers declared his Double Concerto 1 for two violins to be the outstanding composition of the year in 1959. He was appointed foreign member of the Royal Academy of Sciences, Literature, and Arts of Belgium in 1949, and was given honorary citizenship of the city of New Martinsville, West Virginia, U.S., in 1965. Other prizes and distinctions include the Johan Wagenaar Prize in 1967, the Sweelinck Prize from the Dutch Government for his total *oeuvre* in 1972, the medal of Arts-Sciences-lettre de l'Académie Française in 1981, Prize of the Dutch for Winds in 1984, and the Medaille de la Jeunesse Musicale of the Northern Netherlands in 1985. The prize for the best European choral composition (*Missa Antiphonica*) was awarded posthumously in 1988.

Henk Badings died on 26 June 1987 at his country home, "Hugten," near Maarheeze at the southern border of the Netherlands, where he lived the last fifteen years of his life.

ABBREVIATIONS

A	=	alto
al lib	=	ad libitum
arp	=	harp
B	=	bass
bar	=	baritone
CSP	=	*Cantiones sacrae et profanae* (7 volumes) published by Harmonia
cb	=	double bass
cel	=	celeste
ch	=	choir
cor	=	French horn
cor ingl	=	English horn
dur	=	duration
el magn	=	electromagnetic
el mus	=	electronic music
euph	=	euphonium
fg	=	bassoon
fl	=	flute
guit	=	guitar
glock	=	glockenspiel

hph	=	heckelphone or baritone-oboe
instr	=	instrumentation
lyr	=	lyrical
nar	=	narrator
ob	=	oboe
ob d'am	=	oboe d'amore
obl	=	obbligato
org	=	organ
pf	=	pianoforte
perc	=	percussion
S	=	soprano
sax	=	saxophone
str. 5	=	string quintet or string orchestra
T	=	tenor
timp	=	timpani
tr	=	trumpet
trbn	=	trombone
tub	=	tuba
vl	=	violin
vla	=	viola
vlc	=	violoncello
vol	=	volume

INSTRUMENTATION CODE

In the indication 2222 - 4 sax (2atb) - 4330 - timp, perc, cb, str. 5 the first four ciphers are related to the woodwind family in the order flute, oboe, clarinet and bassoon; the saxophones are only mentioned if used (in this example, 2 alto, 1 tenor, and 1 baritone saxophone); in the second group the four ciphers are related to the brass in the order horns, trumpets, trombones, tubas (in this example no tubas), timpani, percussion; cb means that only the double bass is used. This indication for double bass will appear frequently in compositions for wind orchestra and other chamber ensembles. The full string orchestra is announced as str. 5 (including double bass).

PUBLISHERS

(A)   Alsbach and Co.; now: le Muziekcentrale, Ambachtsweg 42, 1271 AM Huizen, Netherlands

(AB)   Albersen, Groot Hertoginnelaan 182, 2517 EV Den Haag, Netherlands

(BA)   Annie Bank (see Harmonia address)

(BE)   Beiaardschool, Mechelen, Belgium

(BER) Ed. Berbèn, 60100 Ancona, Italy

(BH)   Boosey and Hawkes, London, England

(BP)   Broekmans and van Poppel, v. Baerlestraat 92-94, 1071 BB Amsterdam, Netherlands

(DO)   Donemus, Paulus Potterstraat 15, 1071 CZ Amsterdam, Netherlands

(EFN) European Musical Festival for the Youth, Stationstraat 25, 3580 Neerpelt, Belgium

(EG)   Engstrom and Soldring Musikforlag, Palaisgade 6, 1261 Kobenhavn, Denmark

(EH)   De Muziekerije (Ed. Heuwekemeyer), Groest 112, 1211 EE Hilversum, Netherlands

(HARM)	Harmonia, Postbus 210, 1230 AE Loosdrecht, Netherlands
(HO)	Ed. Hohner, Trossingen, Germany
(LEU)	Leuckart Musikverlag, 8000 München, Germany
(LTC)	Lichtenauer, Kruisplein 44, 3012 CC Rotterdam, Netherlands
(LO)	Lester and Orpen, Toronto, Canada
(KZCB)	Postbus 64, 2250 AB Voorschoten, Netherlands
(KNZB)	KoNeZa, Postbus 2255, 6430 AG Hoensbroek, Netherlands
(MO)	Molenaar, Industrieweg 23, 1521 ND Wormerveer, Netherlands
(Ms.)	Manuscript, Henk Badings Foundation, Hugten 5, 6026 RG Maarheeze, Netherlands
(MV)	Moeck Musikverlag, Celle, Germany
(P)	C. F. Peters Corp., 373 Park Avenue South, New York, NY 10016, U.S.
(SM)	Ed. Schott, Weihergarten 5, Mainz, Germany
(SCHU)	Ed. Schultz, am Märchengrabe 6, 7800 Greiburg-Tiengen, Germany
(SO)	Sofirad; now: Ed. Francaises de Musique, Office de Radio-Diffusion et Television Française, 116 Av. de Pont Kennedy, Paris, France 16
(SP)	Shawnee Press, Inc., Delaware Watergap, PA 18327, U.S.
(UE)	Universal Edition, Karlsplatz 6, Wien, Austria
(WH)	Wilhelm Hansen Musikforleg, Copenhagen, Denmark
(Z)	Zomer en Keunings, Wageningen, Netherlands

Electronic tapes can be rented from the Henk Badings Foundation, Hugten 5, 6026 RG Maarheeze, Netherlands

Henk Badings, 1907-87

Catalog of Works

1 COMPOSITIONS FOR PIANO

Solo

Adagio 1954 (Ms.) dur. 2′   **W-1**

Adagio cantabile 1967 (DO) dur. 10′   **W-2**

Arcadia
Little Pieces for Beginners   **W-3**
Dedication: Hetty Badings
(See p. 7 for vols. 4-5, 8)

Volume 1 1945 (SM) dur. 10′   **W-3a**
      1. Canon; 2. Canto chorale; 3. Basso ostinato;
      4. Cavalleresco; 5. Canon; 6. Scherzo; 7. Inter-
      mezzo; 8. Canon; 9. Ballo; 10. Rondo finale

Volume 2 1945 (SM) dur. 10′   **W-3b**
      1. Intonazione; 2. Arietta; 3. Rigodon; 4. Scherzo;
      5. Intermezzo; 6. Valser; 7. Elegia; 8. Ballo
      contadinesco; 9. Siciliano; 10. Galoppo finale

Volume 3 1945 (SM) dur. 15′   **W-3c**
      1. Sarabande; 2. Burlesca; 3. Canto esotico;
      4. Tamburino; 5. Notturno; 6. Valser; 7. Fanfare;
      8. Ballo orientale; 9. Scherzo; 10. Rondo finale

Arcadia - (*continued*)

Volume 6   1967 (DO)   dur. 12'   **W-3f**
     1. Bicinium; 2. Passepied; 3. Epigram;
     4. Nocturne; 5. Wals; 6. Romance; 7. Xenogram;
     8. Indizio

Volume 7   1967 (DO)   dur. 23'   **W-3g**
     1. Incanto; 2. Dialogo; 3. Xenie; 4. Evocazione;
     5. Monologo; 6. Xenogram; 7. Fantasia;
     8. Postludium

Boogie Woogie   1059 (HARM)   dur 1'   **W-4**

Canarie   1974 (Ms.)   dur. 2'   **W-5**

Drie kleine klavierstukken   1951   (Ms.)   dur. 5'   **W-6**
(Three Little Piano Pieces)
     1. Andante; 2. Allegro; 3. Largo
     Dedication: Eduard Flipse

Fünf kleine Klavierstücke   1983 (SM)   dur. 7'30''   **W-7**
(Five Little Piano Pieces)
     1. Zwei Reiter; 2. Bauerntanz; 3. Reel;
     4. Sarabande triste; 5. Walzer in schwarz und
     weiss
     Commission: Schott Music Co.

Images de Noël   1982 (DO)   dur. 8'   **W-8**
     1. Prévisions; 2. Avant des âmes simples;
     3. Berceuse; 4. Adoration
     Dedication: Cor de Groot

La megicana   1978 (Ms.)   dur. 6'   **W-9**
     Dedication: Helmut Schoell

Quaderni sonori   1976 (DO)   dur. 24'   **W-10**
     1. Preludio; 2. Ciacona; 3. Interludio; 4. Notturno
     5. Etude; 6. Scherzo; 7. Postludio
     Dedication: Helmut Schoell
     Premiere: 17 January 1977, Stuttgart, Germany;
     soloist: Hellmut Schoell

Passacaglia (Theme with Eight Variations) 1979 (Ms.)   **W-11**
   dur. 7'30''
      Dedication: Hellmut Schoell

Passacaglia on BESC 1982 (Ms.)   dur. 3'   **W-12**
      Commission: Foundation of the Southern
       Historic Union

Prelude 1949 (Ms.)   dur. 1'   **W-13**
      Commission: Elsevier

Reihe kleiner Klavierstücke 1939 (SM)   dur. 12'   **W-14**
(Series of Little Piano Pieces) for beginners
      1. Intrada; 2. Siciliano; 3. Ballo guio; 4. Air;
      5. Rondo popolare; 6. Menuet; 7. Scherzo
      pastorale; 8. Rondo finale
      Dedication: Vera

Roemeense reisschetsen 1935 (DO)   dur. 15'   **W-15**
(Romanian Traveling Sketches)
      1. Predilcova; 2. Gaura Lupilor; 3. Cruzea Verde;
      4. Fata Mare; 5. Magura Thema with 10 variations
      Dedication: Felix de Nobel

Sonata 1 1934 (SM)   dur. 15'   **W-16**
      1. Allegro; 2. Largo; 3. Scherzo presto; 4. Vivace
      Dedication: Prof. Dr. Ir. J. A. A. Mekel

Sonata 2 1941 (SM)   dur. 15'   **W-17**
      1. Allegro; 2. Largo; 3. Presto

Sonata 3 1944 (DO)   dur. 12'   **W-18**
      1. Allegro; 2. Lento; 3. Allegretto

Sonata 4 1945 (WH)   dur. 10'   **W-19**
      1. Allegro molto; 2. Con moto; 3. Presto
      Dedication: Cor de Groot

Sonata 5 1945 (A)   dur. 9'   **W-20**
      1. Presto; 2. Largo; 3. Vivace
      Dedication: Hetty Badings

Sonata 6 1947 (DO)   dur. 24'   **W-21**
  1. Allegro; 2. Adagio; 3. Scherzo; 4. Rondo
  Dedication: Cor de Groot

Sonatina 1 1936 (SM)   dur. 10'   **W-22**
  1. Allegro; 2. Andante; 3. Allegro Vivace
  Dedication: Felix de Nobel

Sonatina 2 1945 (DO)   dur. 6'   **W-23**
  1. Allegro; 2. Andante; 3. Presto

Sonatina 3 1950 (DO)   dur. 5'   **W-24**
  1. Arabesco (con moto); 2. Canzonetta (adagio);
  3. Epilogo (moderato)
  Commission: Bender
  Premiere: 12 October 1950, Amsterdam, by
    Schouwmann

Sonatina 4 1958 (HARM)   dur. 6'   **W-25**
  1. Molto allegro; 2. Cantabile; 3. Presto

Suite   1930 (DO)   dur. 10'   **W-26**
  1. Preludium; 2. Aria; 3. Fughetta; 4. Lento;
  5. Rondo

Tema con variazioni   1938 (UE)   dur. 12'   **W-27**
  Dedication: Stien and Henk Resser

Variations à la manière de . . .   1951 (Ms.)   dur. 6'   **W-28**
  1. Couperin (La Tendre Portense de l'eau); 2. Mozart
  (Allegretto grazioso); 3. Händel (Sarabande);
  4. Chopin (Polonaise); 5. Debussy (La Fille aux
  sabots blancs); 6. Beethoven (Allegro für das
  Hammerklavier)
  Commission: Elsevier

Vijf kleine klavierstukken   1967 (DO)   dur. 8'   **W-29**
  (Five Little Piano Pieces)
  1. Preludio; 2. Fantasia; 3. Punto d'orgue; 4.
  Xeno
  gramma; 5. Epilogo

Wals   1953 (Ms.)   dur. 1'   **W-30**
  (Waltz)
  Commission: Elsevier

Xenie   1958 (HARM)   dur. 1'   **W-31**

Four Hands/Two Pianos

Arcadia
Little Pieces for Beginners
Dedication: Hetty Badings
(See pp. 3-4 for vols. 1-3, 6-7)

Volume 4 (four hands) 1945 (SM) dur. 10′ **W-3d**
1. Preludium; 2. Orgelpunkt; 3. Intermezzo;
4. Elegie; 5. Tripla; 6. Scherzo; 7. Menuet;
8. Siciliano; 9. Ballade; 10. Finale
Dedication: Hetty Badings

Volume 5 (four hands) 1945 (SM) dur. 10′ **W-3e**
1. Preludio; 2. Sarabande; 3. Canzonetta;
4. Elegia; 5. Cinque fonte di picche; 6. Mazurka;
7. Enigma; 8. Illusione; 9. Giochetto; 10. Rondo
finale

Volume 8 (four hands) 1967 (SM) dur. 13′ **W-3h**
1. Foxtrot; 2. Dialogo; 3. Canto primaverile;
4. Notturno; 5. Caccia; 6. Illusione

Balletto grottesco 1939 (UE) (two pianos) dur. 10′ **W-32**
1. Intrada; 2. Marcia funèbre; 3. Ballo;
4. Intermezzo; 5. Rondo populare; 6. Rumba

Balletto notturno 1975 (DO) (two pianos) dur. 12′ **W-33**
1. Giaoco delle compane lontane (Molto moderato);
2. Giaoco degli arabeschi sinnuosi (Lento)
Dedication: Helmut Schoell
Premiere: 17 January 1977, Stuttgart, Germany

Balleto serioso 1955 (DO) (two pianos) dur. 25′ **W-34**
1. Introduzione (Lento); 2. Tempo di valse;
3. Tema con variazione; 4. Tempo di valse;
5. Largo (Sarabande); 6. Marcia; 7. Aria; 8. Coda
Commission: Johan Wagenaar Foundation

Beguine 1978 (Ms.) (four hands) dur. 3′ **W-35**
Dedication: Ru Sevenhuysen - 25th wedding
anniversary
(*See* Chamber Music/Other Combinations - **W-129**)

Foxtrot   1955 (Ms.)   **W-36**

Two Grotesken   1927 (Ms.)   (two pianos)   **W-37**
      1. Moderato; 2. Lento

With Electronic Sound

Concertino   1967 (DO)   **W-38**
      for piano and two electronic sound tracks   dur. 10′
         Dedication: Hellmut Schoell

Kontrapunkte   1970   **W-39**
      in collaboration with Hellmut Schoell (Ms.)
      for piano and tape (one track)   dur. 15′

2   COMPOSITIONS FOR OTHER SOLO INSTRUMENTS

VIOLIN

Sonata 1   1940 (SM)   dur. 14′   **W-40**
      1. Allegro; 2. Adagio; 3. Allegretto

Sonata 2   1951 (DO)   dur. 15′   **W-41**
      1. Allegro molto; 2. Adagio; 3. Presto
      Dedication: Queen of the Arts, Elizabeth of
         Belgium
      Award: Paganini Prize, Genoa, Italy (1953)
      Premiere: September 1957, Genoa

Sonata 3 1951 (SM)   dur. 15' W-42
1. Allegro; 2. Largo; 3. Allegro
Dedication: Paul Hindemith (in remembrance)
Award: Paganini Prize, Genoa, Italy (1953)
Premiere: September 1957, Genoa

VIOLONCELLO

Sonata 1 1941 (SM)   dur. 16' W-43
1. Allegro; 2. Adagio; 3. Allegro

Sonata 2 1951 (DO)   dur. 10' W-44
1. Allegro; 2. Grave; 3. Presto
Premiere: 19 November 1951, The Hague;
    by Blattman

GUITAR

Preambolo, Aria e Postludio   1985 (DO)   dur. 4' W-45
Dedication: Piero Bonaguri

Twelve Preludes 1961 (BER)   dur. 24' W-46
1. Intrada; 2. Interludio; 3. Canon; 4. Yaya;
5. Tricinium; 6. Utopia; 7. Fuga; 8. Bicinium;
9. Scherzo; 10. Arpeggio; 11. Canzonetta;
12. Rasquendo
Commission: City of Amsterdam

HARP

Sonata   1944 (DO)   dur. 12' W-47
1. Allegro; 2. Lento; 3. Allegretto

MARIMBAPHONE

Toccata   1973 (DO)   dur. 7' W-48
Dedication: Matsiko Takahashi
Premiere: 1973, Tokyo, Japan, by Takahashi

ACCORDION

Sonata   1981 (DO)   dur. 15'   **W-49**
    1. Prologo; 2. Episodio dramatico; 3. Arioso;
    4. Giocoso; 5. Epilogo
    Commission: Dutch Government

3   CHAMBER MUSIC

Duets

VIOLIN AND PIANO

Air triste   1947 (DO)   dur. 8'   **W-50**
    Dedication: Carel van Leeuwen Boomkamp
    Premiere: Radio Paris

Capriccio   1936 (SM)   dur. 6'   **W-51**
    Dedication: Zoltan Székely

Cavatina   1952 (DO)   dur. 5'   **W-52**

The Fiddler and His Mate   1945 (HARM)   **W-53**
    Little Pieces for Beginners

    Volume 1   dur. 6'
        1. Aeolus Harp; 2. Lenteliedje; 3. Bezwering
        4. Elegie; 5. Elfenwals

    Volume 2   dur. 6'   **W-53b**
        1. Berceuse; 2. Kabounterdans; 3. Air;
        4. Kabouterconcert

Volume 3   dur. 6'   **W-53c**
    1. Elfenharp; 2. Wals; 3. Burleske; 4. Arietta;
    5. Scherzo

Volume 4   dur. 9'   **W-53d**
    1. Elfendans; 2. Kobold vertelt; 3. Kobold danst;
    4. De vogel met de gouden veren; 5. Algemeene
    rondedans

Romance   1957 (DO)   dur. 2'   **W-54**

Rondino   1960 (BP)   dur. 2'   **W-55**

Sonata   1928 (Ms.)   dur. 10'   **W-56**
    1. Allegro; 2. Lento; 3. Allegro vivo

Sonata 1   1933 (SM)   dur. 15'   **W-57**
    1. Allegro; 2. Adagio; 3. Allegro vivace
    Commission: ISCM, Prague

Sonata 2   1939 (SM)   dur. 15'   **W-58**
    1. Allegro molto; 2. Andante; 3. Allegro
    Dedication: Eugene Calkoen

Sonata 3   1952 (DO)   dur. 20'   **W-59**
    1. Allegro; 2. Canzona; 3. Rondo giocoso
    Dedication: Rudolf Mengelberg
    Premiere: 17 October 1952, Amsterdam by Nicolas
       Roth and R. V. Mill

Sonata 4   1931 (DO)   dur. 15'   **W-60**
    1. Allegro; 2. Adagio; 3. Allegro molto

Sonata 5   1984 (DO)   dur. 17'   **W-61**
    1. Introduzione, lento-presto; 2. Adagio appassionato
    3. Finale scherzando
    Dedication: Peter Zakofsky
    Premiere: New York, Peter Zakofsky

Xenie   1959 (BP)   dur. 1'   **W-62**

VIOLA AND PIANO

Cavatina   1952 (DO)   dur. 5'   **W-63**
    Dedication: L. Dolstra

Sonata   1951 (DO)   dur. 17′   W-64
      1. Allegro; 2. Largo; 3. Vivace
      Dedication: L. Dolstra
      Premiere: December 1951

VIOLONCELLO AND PIANO

Sonata 1   1929 (DO)   dur. 15′   W-65
      1. Allegro; 2. Lento moderato; 3. Allegro vivace
      Dedication: Sigtenhorst Meyer
      Premiere: Amsterdam Concertgebouw

Sonata 2   1934 (A)   dur. 15′   W-66
      1. Allegro molto; 2. Adagio; 3. Allegro vivace

Vier voordrachtstukken   1946 (DO)   dur. 18′   W-67
(Four Recital Pieces)
      1. Serenade; 2. Scherzo pizzicato; 3. Air triste;
      4. Rondo giocoso
      Premiere: Radio Paris

FLUTE AND PIANO

Capriccio   1936 (DO)   dur. 6′   W-68

OBOE AND PIANO

Cavatina   1952 (DO)   dur. 5′   W-69

Sonata   1929 (Ms.)   dur. 15′   W-70
      1. Allegro; 2. Lento non troppo; 3. Allegro assai

ALTO SAXOPHONE AND PIANO

Cavatina   1952 (DO)   dur. 5′   W-71

La malinconia   1949 (DO)   dur. 8′   W-72
      Dedication: Sigurd Rascher
      Premiere: U.S. by Sigurd Rascher

Largo cantabile   1983 (DO)   dur. 6′   W-73
    Dedication: Dorene and David Bilger
    Premiere: U.S.

HARMONICA AND PIANO

Blues   1957 (HO)   dur. 5′   W-74

TWO VIOLINS

Kleine Duetten   1945 (DO)   dur. 15′   W-75
(Little Duets for pupil and teacher)
    1. Preludium; 2. Rondino; 3. Scherzo; 4. Tambourin
    5. Intermezzo; 6. Grave; 7. Ballo furioso; 8. Arietta
    9. Ritorno ostinato; 10. Serenata

Kleine Suite   1948 (DO)   dur. 6′   W-76
(Little Suite)
    1. Preludium; 2. Scherzo; 3. Sarabande; 4. Finale
    Commission: Dutch Railroad

Quick Step   1960 (BP)   dur. 1′30″   W-77

Sonata 1   1928 (DO)   dur. 10′   W-78
    1. Allegro; 2. Lento; 3. Allegro

Sonata 2   1963 (DO)   dur. 16′   W-79
(in the 31-tone temperament)
    1. Lento-vivace; 2. Molto adagio; 3. Vivace
    Commission: Society for Precise Listening
    Dedication: "Duo Lemkes"
    Premiere: 1 October 1967, Haarlem by "Duo
      Lemkes"

Sonata 3   1967 (DO)   dur. 9′   W-80
(in the 31-tone temperament)
    1. Lento; 2. Molto allegro; 3. Finale
    Dedication: Duo Lemkes
    Premiere: 1967, Haarlem, by "Duo Lemkes"

Sonata 4 1975 (DO) dur. 16′   **W-81**
(Variations on Seikilos' Skolion)
(in the 31-tone temperament)
>   1. Introduction; 2. Thema; 3. Variations;
>   4. Passacaglia
>   *Dedication:* "Duo Lemkes"
>   *Premiere:* 4 April 1976, Haarlem, by "Duo
>   Lemkes"

Sonata 5 1981 (DO) dur. 17′   **W-82**
(in the 31-tone temperament)
>   1. Réflections; 2. Evocations; 3. Danse finale
>   *Commission:* Huygens-Fokker Foundation
>   *Dedication:* "Duo Lemkes"
>   *Premiere:* 1981, Haarlem, by "Duo Lemkes"

Sonata 6 1984 (DO) dur. 12′   **W-83**
(in the 31-tone temperament)
>   1. Lento-con moto; 2. Arioso; 3. Finale
>   *Dedication:* "Duo Lemkes"
>   *Premiere:* 1984, Haarlem, by "Duo Lemkes"

VIOLIN AND VIOLA

Sonata 1928 (DO) dur. 12′   **W-84**
>   1. Allegro; 2. Andante; 3. Allegro

VIOLIN AND VIOLONCELLO

Sonata 1927 (DO) dur. 10′   **W-85**
>   1. Moderato; 2. Andante; 3. Vivace

VIOLIN AND GUITAR

Variations 1983 (DO) dur. 12′   **W-86**
>   *Commission:* Kristen Bennion
>   *Dedication:* Douglas Hensley
>   *Premiere:* 1983, San Francisco, U.S., by Douglas
>   Hensley and Kristen Bennion

VIOLIN AND RECORDER

Suite 2 1957 (HARM) dur. 6' W-87
1. Preludium; 2. Scherzo; 3. Sarabande; 4. Finale

VIOLIN AND TAPE (2 SOUND TRACKS)

Capriccio 1959 (DO) dur. 7'30'' W-88
Commission: Ir. J. Vermeulen
Premiere: 1959, Amsterdam

FLUTE AND GUITAR

Sonata 1983 (DO) dur. 14' W-89
1. Capriccio; 2. Cadenza; 3. Notturno; 4. Rondo
giocoso
Dedication: Douglas Hensley
Premiere: 1983, San Francisco, U.S., by Douglas
   Hensley

FLUTE AND HARP

Ballade 1950 (DO) dur. 17' W-90
1. Lento; 2. Allegro; 3. Meno mosso; 4. Vivace
Commission and Dedication: H. Barwahser and
   Phia Berghout
Premiere: 22 August 1950, Maatstricht

Sonata 1982 (DO) dur. 18' W-91
1. Improvisation; 2. Scherzo; 3. Grave; 4. Finale
Commission: Dutch Government

ALTO FLUTE AND HARP

Cavatina 1952 (DO) dur. 5' W-92

RECORDER AND HARPSICHORD

Sonata 1957 (DO) dur. 15' W-93
1. Allegro; 2. Adagio; 3. Andante
Commission: Höhner, Germany

TWO RECORDERS

Suite 1   1950 (EH)   dur. 5'   W-94
           1. Preludio; 2. Ballo; 3. Arietta; 4. Scherzino
           5. Sarabande; 6. Rondo finale

Suite 3   1958 (HARM)   dur. 5'   W-95
    (can be played with three players)
           1. Lento; 2. Vivace; 3. Grazioso; 4. Presto

THREE RECORDERS

Suite 2   1958 (HARM)   dur. 5'   W-96
    (can be played with two players)
           1. Lento; 2. Vivace; 3. Grazioso; 4. Presto

TRUMPET AND TAPE (1 SOUND-TRACK)

Chaconne   1965 (DO)   dur. 12'   for B-flat trumpet   W-97
           Introduction - Chaconne Variations - Intermezzo -
           Chaconne Variations - Epilogue - Finale
           Dedication: Robert Boudreau

Trios

Trio 1   1934 (SM)   dur. 20'   for vl, vlc, pf   W-98
           1. Allegro; 2. Adagio; 3. Scherzo presto 4. Allegro
           vivace
           Premiere: 1934, ISCM, Paris, France

Trio 2   1943 (DO)   dur. 16'   for ob, cl, fg   W-99
           1. Allegro; 2. Scherzo; 3. Theme con Variazioni;
           4. Rondo allegro
           Premiere: 1934, Brussels, Belgium

Trio 3   1945 (DO)   dur. 12'   for 2 vl, vla   W-100
           1. Allegro; 2. Lento; 3. Presto
           Dedication: Darius Milhaud

Trio 4 1946 (DO)   dur. 12'   for 2 ob, cor ingl; other   **W-101**
version - 3 vl
  1. Allegro giocoso; 2. Canto armouroso; 3. Rondino
  scherzando
  Dedication: Carel van Leeuwen Boomkamp

Trio 5 1947 (DO)   dur. 14'   for fl, vl, vla   **W-102**
  1. Allegro; 2. Allegretto grazioso; 3. Allegro
  vivace
  Dedication: Francesco Malipiero

Trio 6 1951 (DO)   dur. 17'   for 2 vl, pf   **W-103**
  1. Molto allegro; 2. Largo
  Dedication: H. v. d. Vegt (in memoriam)
  Premiere: The Hague, by "Trio Hansen"

Trio 7 1953 (DO)   dur. 17'   for 2 vl, vla   **W-104**
  1. Allegro; 2. Scherzo (vivace); 3. Adagietto;
  4. Presto

Trio 8 1955 (MV)   dur. 5'   for 3 recorders   **W-105**
  1. Fughetta; 2. Con moto moderato; 3. Passacaglia
  Commission: Moeck Verlag

Trio 9 1962 (DO)   dur. 17'   for fl, vla, guit   **W-106**
  1. Lento; 2. Allegro; 3. Adagio; 4. Scherzo
  Premiere: 13 February 1962, Paris, France

Trio 10 1977 (DO)   dur. 16'   for alto fl, vla, arp   **W-107**
  1. Lento; 2. Scherzo (presto); 3. Grave
  Commission: Dutch Government
  Dedication: Netherlands Harp Ensemble
  Premiere: 19 January 1978, by "Trio P. Ode"

Trio 11 1981 (DO)   dur. 15'   for 2 vl, archiphone   **W-108**
  (in the 31-tone temperament)
  (can be played with 2 violins)
    1. Demonstration; 2. Air; 3. Improvisation
    Commission: Huygens-Fokker Foundation
    Dedication: Bouw Lemkes and Jeanne Vos

Trio 12 1986 (DO)   dur. 15'   for cl, cor ingl, fg   **W-109**
    1. Tranquillo - Allegro molto; 2. Arioso; 3. Finale
    Commission: Dorothy Darlington
    Premiere: 17 August 1991, Baltimore, U.S., for
      the International Double Reed Society

Trios Cosmos   1981-82 (SM)   **W-110**
   16 trios for amateur violin groups from beginning to
      advanced levels (see *Educational Music*)
   All commissioned by the Dutch Government

   Trio 1   dur. 7'30''   **W-110a**
      1. Canon; 2. Walzer; 3. Sarabande; 4. Musette
      Dedication: Yvonne Badings

   Trio 2   dur. 9'30''   **W-110b**
      1. Introduction; 2. Waltz; 3. Musing; 4. Sword
      Dance
      Dedication: Hans Zijderlaan

   Trio 3   dur. 11'   **W-110c**
      1. Primavera; 2. Perpetuum mobile; 3. Dance for
      the Nymphs; 4. Czardas; 5. Amarant
      Dedication: Piet't Hart

   Trio 4   dur. 8'30''   **W-110d**
      1. Nostalgia; 2. Japanese Song; 3. American Song;
      4. Japanese Song
      Dedication: Cor van Iersel

   Trio 5   dur. 8'   **W-110e**
      1. Pensieroso (canon); 2. Inno lydico; 3. Mottetto
      serio; 4. Romanza
      Dedication: Jeanne Vos

   Trio 6   dur. 12'   **W-110f**
      1. Unisono and Canon; 2. Bourée; 3. Phrygisches
      Menuett; 4. Fuga giocosa
      Dedication: Bouw Lemkes

   Trio 7   dur. 12'30''   **W-110g**
      1. Marksman's March; 2. Melancholic Romance;
      3. Rigaudon Rotterdam; 4. Tempo di mazurka
      Dedication: Peet Scheymans

   Trio 8   dur. 12'30''   **W-110h**
      1. Mars; 2. Scherzo pastorale; 3. Aria (Song of the
      Nightingale); 4. Pulcinella
      Dedication: Piet and Lidy Vullinghs

   Trio 9   dur. 11'30''   **W-110i**
      1. Habanera; 2. Foxtrot; 3. Blues; 4. Charleston
      Dedication: Richard Wurster

Trio 10   dur. 12'30''   **W-110j**
    1. Rousing Ragtime; 2. Boston; 3. Desolate Blues;
    4. Cheerful Tango

Trio 11   dur. 14'   **W-110k**
    1. Tucker's March; 2. Canon on Pizzicato Ostinato;
    3. Melicious Sarabande; 4. Louré
    Dedication: Jean Laurent

Trio 12   dur. 13'   **W-110l**
    1. Prelude for a Sad Princess; 2. Spinner's Air of
    Brabant; 3. Arietta seria; 4. Giga finale
    Dedication: Hetty Badings

Trio 13   dur. 14'   **W-110m**
    1. Gaillarde Roemer; 2. Chaconne; 3. Rigaudon;
    4. Pretty Isabel
    Dedication: Ru Sevenhuysen

Trio 14   dur. 12'30''   **W-110n**
    1. Furioso; 2. Volante; 3. Elegie on the G-String;
    4. Finale on the E-String
    Dedication: Gisela Schwanke

Trio 15   1983   dur. 15' (Advanced Level)   **W-110o**
    1. Improvisation on One Note; 2. Improvisation
    on Two Notes; 3. Improvisation on Three or More
    Notes; 4. Improvisation on Many Notes and
    Graphic Notation

Trio 16   1984   dur. 15'   **W-110p**
    1. Lento - Molto vivace; 2. Adagietto; 3. Presto
    Dedication: Coosje Wijzenbeek

Quartets

Drie Nederlandse dansen   1950 (LI)   dur. 10'   for 2 tr, cor, trbn   **W-111**
(Three Dutch Dances)
    1. Hollandse boerenplof (Dutch Farmer's Dance);
    2. Gelderse peerdesprong (Gelderse Horse's Jump);
    3. Friese trye (Friese Dance)

Koperkwartet   1947 (DO)   dur. 12′   for 2 tr, cor, trbn   W-112
(Brass Quartet)
>   1. Intrada; 2. Scherzo; 3. Canzonetta; 4. Rondo
>   giocoso

Oboe Quartet   *Variations on the Bluetail-fly*   1975 (P)   dur. 7′   W-113
for ob, ob d'am, cor. ingl, hph
>   Var. 1, Tranquillo; var. 2, Agitato; var. 3, Rubato;
>   var. 4, Andante (siciliano); var. 5, Agitato

Piano Quartet   1973 (DO)   dur. 18′   for vl, vla, vlc, pf   W-114
>   1. Lento dappoi presto; 2. Adagio; 3. Allegro molto
>   *Commission:* Dutch Government

Seven Quartets for Instruments at Pleasure   1978   W-115
Instrumental options:
>   A. recorder satb; B. 3 fl, 1 alto fl; C. 3 ob, 1 cor
>   ingl; D. 4 cl; E. 3 alto sax, 1 ten sax; F. 1 sop
>   sax, 2 alto sax, 1 ten sax; G. 3 vl, 1 vla
>   (*See* Educational Music)

Quartet 1   (HARM)   dur. 9′   W-115a
>   1. Gagliarde gaia; 2. Minuetto multiplo; 3. Aria
>   seria; 4. Giga giocosa

Quartet 2   (HARM)   dur. 12′   W-115b
>   1. Canario; 2. Mazurka; 3. Paso doble; 4. Pavanne

Quartet 3   (HARM)   dur. 10′   W-115c
>   1. Allegro assai; 2. Molto adagio; 3. Allegro

Quartet 4   (HARM)   dur. 16′   W-115d
>   1. Improvisation on One Note; 2. Improvisation
>   on Two Notes; 3. Improvisation on Three or More
>   Notes; 4. Improvisation on Many Notes and
>   Graphic Notation

Quartet 5   (HARM)   dur. 13′   W-115e
>   1. Marcia lieta; 2. Arioso serio; 3. Valzer strano;
>   4. Tango popolare

Quartet 6   (Schu)   dur. 15′   W-115f
>   1. Signale; 2. Narrentans im Elfertahl; 3. Melancholie;
>   4. Fughetta and potpourri
>   *Commission:* Schulz Publishing Co., Freiburg

Quartet 7 (HARM) dur. 12'
    1. La ostinata; 2. La ragazza di Santa Cruz; 3. La
pensosa; 4. Finale la creola
                                                          W-115g

String Quartet 1929 (Ms.)   **W-116**
    1. Allegro vivace; 2. Lento non troppo; 3. Allegro
assai

String Quartet 1 1931 (SM) dur. 15'   **W-117**
    1. Allegro; 2. Presto; 3. Adagio; 4. Allegro molto
Award: Netherlands Prize (1935)
Commission: ISCM
Dedication: Prof. H. F. Grondijs
Premiere: Warsaw, Poland

String Quartet 2 1936 (SM) dur. 15'   **W-118**
    1. Allegro; 2. Scherzo presto; 3. Adagio; 4. Allegro
vivace
Dedication: New Hungarian String Quartet

String Quartet 3 1944 (DO) dur. 21'   **W-119**
    1. Allegro; 2. Scherzo; 3. Adagio; 4. Rondo
Premiere: 1 March 1948, by Röntgen Quartet

String Quartet 4 1966 (DO) dur. 20'   **W-120**
  (in the 31-tone temperament)
    1. Lento; 2. Allegro; 3. Adagio; 4. Vivace
Commission: Huygens Fokker Foundation

String Quartet 5 1980 (DO) dur. 25'   **W-121**
    1. Tema e introduzione; 2. Impetuoso; 3. Mesto;
4. Giocoso
Commission: Johan Wagenaar Foundation
Premiere: 29 April 1881, Amsterdam, by Orlando
Quartet

Quintets

Quintet 1 1928 (DO) dur. 15' for fl, cl, vl, vla, vlc   **W-122**
    1. Allegro; 2. Lento non troppo; 3. Allegro

Quintet 2 1929 (DO) dur. 15′ for fl, ob, cl, fag, cor   **W-123**
1. Allegro; 2. Adagio; 3. Allegro
Premiere: 1929, The Hague

Quintet 3 *Capriccio* 1936 (DO) dur. 6′ for fl, vl, vla,   **W-124**
  vlc, arp

Quintet 4 1948 (DO) dur. 25′ for fl, ob, cl, fag, cor   **W-125**
1. Allegro; 2. Molto adagio; 3. Scherzo; 4. Allegro
Dedication: Concertgebouw Quartet
Premiere: 1 July 1949, by Concertgebouw Quartet

Quintet 5 1952 (DO) dur. 24′ for pf, 2 vl, vla, vlc   **W-126**
1. Allegro; 2. Scherzo presto; 3. Adagio e mesto;
4. Rondo allegro vivace
Award: Academia Chigiani Prize, Siena, Italy (1952)
Premiere: 1952, Venice

Quintet 6 1985 (DO) dur. 16′ for cl, vl, vcl, guit, arp   **W-127**
1. Cappriccio; 2. Serioso; 3. Giocoso
Dedication: Douglas Hensley

Other Combinations

Azioni musicali 1980 (DO) dur. 24′; instr. 2222-2000 - vlc, cb   **W-128**
1. Serioso; 2. Scherzo; 3. Variazoni concertanti
Dedication: "Octopus"

Beguine 1978 (Ms.) dur. 3′00″ for four treble instr., bass,   **W-129**
  perc, pf
Dedication: Ru Sevenhuysen (25th wedding
  anniversary)
(for *Four Hands/Two Pianos* - **W-35**)

Octet 1952 (DO) dur. 25′ for cl, fag, cor, 2 vl, vla, vlc, ob   **W-130**
1. Allegro; 2. Scherzo (vivace); 3. Thema con
variazoni
Commission and Dedication: Vienna Philharmonic
  Octet
Premiere: 15 June 1952, Holland Festival, Amsterdam
(Arranged by the composer for Wind Ensemble in
  1980)

Sextet 1 *Lentemaan*   1931 (DO)   dur. 8'   for contralto-   **W-131**
voice, fl, cl, vl, vla, vlc
(Spring Moon)
>1. Als uit den hartstocht van het avondrood (Out
>of the passion of the sunset); 2. Ik weet nu zet Uw
>schone deemoed in (Now I); 3. Doove pijnen
>sidderseinen (Trembling)
>(See *Voice(s) with Other Instruments*)

Sextet 2   1952 (DO)   dur. 17'   for fl, ob, cl, fag, cor, pf   **W-132**
>1. Introduzione-burlesco; 2. Adagio; 3. Vivace
>*Premiere:* 3 February 1952, Radio Philharmonic
>   Sextet

Sextet 3   1987 (DO)   dur. 19'   for soprano-voice, fl, cl, vl,   **W-133**
cb, guit
Verses from Tao Teh King by Lao Tsu
>1. The Embodiment of Tao; 2. Praise of Mystery; 3.
>Life in Love; 4. The Genesis of Forms; 5. Warning
>against War
>*Dedication:* Douglas Hensley
>*Premiere:* September 1987, by Ensemble Iskra,
>   San Francisco, U.S.
>(See *Voice(s) with Other Instruments*)

4   ORCHESTRAL WORKS

String Orchestra

Concerto for Viola   1965 (DO)   dur. 18'; instr. str. 5
>(See *Concertos [Symphony Orchestra]* - **W-183**)

Largo und Allegro   1935 (UE)   dur. 12'; instr. str. 5   **W-134**
    Dedication: Bertus van Lier

Serenade   1985 (DO)   dur. 13'; instr. str. 5   **W-135**
    Commission: Dutch Fund for the Creative Arts
    Dedication: Coosje Wijzenbeek

Symphony 9   1960 (DO)   dur. 17'; instr. str. 5
    1. Lento-allegro; 2. Adagio; 3. Allegro
    Commission: Dutch Government
    Dedication: Simon Goldberg
    Premiere: 17 December 1960, Amsterdam,
       1972 version; instr. 0200-2000, str. 5
    (See *Symphony Orchestra* - **W-152**)

Chamber Orchestra

Aria trista e Rondo giocoso   1948 (DO)   dur. 12'; instr.   **W-136**
    1010-000 - arp, pf, str. 5

Concerto for Violoncello 1   1930 (DO)   dur. 15'
    (See *Concertos [Symphony Orchestra]* - **W-189**)

Hora   1935 (DO)   dur. 5'; instr. 1111-1110 - perc, pf, str. 5   **W-137**

Huygens Suite   1987 (HARM)   dur. 15'; instr. 1111-0010 str. 5   **W-138**
    (optional additional instr. 2211 - atb sax - 0010 str. 5 +
    3rd vl)
        1. Overture; 2. Intermezzo; 3. Minuetto and Trio;
        4. Finale
    Commission: Leo Bonebakker
    (See *Mixed Choir with Orchestra*)

Predilcova   1935 (DO)   dur. 5'; instr. 1111-1110 - perc, pf, str. 5   **W-139**

Pupazzetti azzurri   1950 (DO)   dur. 9'; instr. 1120-0220 - bar.   **W-140**
    sax, perc, guit, pf, str. 5
        1. Ragtime; 2. Blues; 3. Tango
    Commission and Dedication: Klaas v. Beek

Rielen   1967 (Ms.)   dur 2'; instr. 1111-1100 - timp, perc, str. 5   **W-141**
    Commission: Dutch Radio

Symphony 1   1932 (DO)   dur. 20'; instr. 2222-2100 - string   **W-142**
    quintet   for 16 solo instruments
        1. Allegro; 2. Largo; 3. Allegro Vivace

Symphonietta   1971 (HARM)   dur. 12'; instr. 2020-0200 -   **W-143**
    timp, str. 5
        1. Allegro vivace; 2. Adagietto; 3. Vivace
        Commission: Harmonia Publishing Co. (Jubilee
          Celebration)
        Premiere: 29 October 1972

Westfriese boeren dans   1967 (Ms.)   dur. 2'; instr. 1111-1100 -   **W-144**
    timp, perc, str. 5
  (Westfriese Farmer's Dance)
        Commission: Dutch Radio

Symphony Orchestra

Symphony 1   1932 (DO)   dur. 20'; instr. 2222-2100 - str. 5
  (See *Chamber Orchestra* - **W-142**)

Symphony 2   1932 (SM)   dur. 20'; instr. 3333-4331 - timp,   **W-145**
    perc, str. 5
        1. Allegro; 2. Adagio; 3. Allegro vivace
        Dedication: Eduard van Beinum
        Premiere: 5 October 1932, Amsterdam,
          Concertgebouw Orchestra

Symphony 3   1934 (UE)   dur. 30'; instr. 3333-4431 - timp,   **W-146**
    perc, str. 5
        1. Allegro; 2. Scherzo presto; 3. Adagio; 4. Allegro
    assai
        Dedication: William Mengelberg
        Premiere: 2 May 1935, Amsterdam, Concertgebouw
    Orchestra

Symphony 4   1943 (DO)   dur. 36'; instr. 3333-4331 - timp,   **W-147**
    perc, cel, str. 5
        1. Lento-allegro; 2. Scherzo presto; 3. Largo e
    mesto; 4. Allegro
        Dedication: Eduard Flipse
        Premiere: 13 October 1947, Rotterdam

Symphony 5 1949 (SM)   dur. 30'; instr. 3333-4331 - timp,   **W-148**
    perc, cel, str. 5
        1. Lento allegro; 2. Scherzo; 3. Largo; 4. Presto
        Award: Prize of the Dutch Government
        Commission and Dedication: Concertgebouw
            Orchestra
        Premiere: 7 December 1949, Concertgebouw
            Orchestra

Symphony 6 *Psalm Symphony* 1953 (DO)   dur. 32'; instr.   **W-149**
    2232-4331 - timp, perc, cel, pf, arp, str. 5 with mixed choir
        1. Lento allegro (Psalm 88); 2. Presto (Psalm 78);
        3. Molto adagio (Psalm 67); 4. Allegro (Psalm 150)
        Commission: Dutch Radio
        Premiere: 25 June 1953, Rotterdam, Holland
            Festival
        (See *Mixed Choir with Symphony Orchestra*)

Symphony 7 *Louisville Symphony* 1954 (DO)   dur. 24';   **W-150**
    instr. 2232-4231 - timp, perc, cel, pf, arp, str. 5
        1. Lento-allegro appassionato; 2. Scherzo-presto;
        3. Adagio; 4. Finale-allegro vivace
        Commission and Dedication: Louisville Symphony
            Orchestra, Robert Whitney, conductor
        Premiere: 26 February 1955, Louisville Symphony
            Orchestra

Symphony 8 *Hannover Symphony* 1956 (DO)   dur. 18';   **W-151**
    instr. 3232-4331 - timp, perc, cel, pf, str. 5
        1. Lento-con moto; 2. Adagietto; 3. Vivace
        Commission: German Radio Corp.
        Premiere: January 11, 1957, Hannover, Germany

Symphony 9 1960 (DO)   dur. 17'; instr. str. 5   **W-152**
        1. Lento-allegro; 2. Adagio; 3. Allegro
        1972 version; instr. 0200-2000, str. 5
        Premiere: Dutch Chamber Orchestra in U.S.,
            Simon Goldberg, conductor
        (See *String Orchestra*)

Symphony 10 1961 (DO)   dur. 22'; instr. 3232-3231 - timp,   **W-153**
    perc, cel, str. 5
        1. Allegro; 2. Presto (scherzo); 3. Adagio; 4. Allegro
        molto
        Commission: City of Rotterdam
        Premiere: 29 January 1962

Symphony 11 *Sinfonia giocosa* 1964 (DO) dur. 8'; instr.   **W-154**
3232-4331 - timp, perc, str. 5 in one movement
> *Commission and Premiere:* City of Eindhoven,
> 26 October 1964

Symphony 12 *Symphonic Sound Patterns* 1964 (DO) dur.   **W-155**
18'; instr. 4343-4331 - timp, perc, arp, cel, pf. str. 5 in
one movement
> *Commission:* Johan Wagenaar Foundation
> *Dedication:* Willem v. Otterloo
> *Premiere:* 20 November 1964, Resident Orchestra
> of The Hague

Symphony 13 1966 (P)
> (See *Wind Orchestra* - **W-221**)

Symphony 14 *Symphonic Triptych* 1968 (DO) dur. 19';   **W-156**
instr. 3333-4331 - timp, perc, cel, str. 5
> 1. Lento; 2. Allegro moderato; 3. Grave
> *Commission:* Festival of Vlaanderen (Belgium)
> *Premiere:* 1 September 1968, Gent

Symphony 15 *Conflicts and Confluences* 1983 (MO)
> (See *Wind Orchestra* - **W-222**)

Other Symphonic Compositions

Balletto serioso 1955 (DO) dur. 25'; instr. 2232-4331 -   **W-157**
timp, perc, cel, pf, str. 5
> 1. Introduzione; 2. Valser; 3. Tema con variazioni;
> 4. Ragtime; 5. Marcia; 6. Air; 7. Epilogo
> *Commission:* Johan Wagenaar Foundation
> *Premiere:* 7 January 1957, Rotterdam
> (See *Four Hands/Two Pianos* - **W-34**)

Concerto for Orchestra 1982 (DO) dur. 21'; instr. 3343-4331 -   **W-158**
timp, perc, str. 5
> 1. Introduction; 2. Scherzo presto; 3. Elegia
> passionata; 4. Finale quodlibet
> At the instigation of Ru Sevenhuysen
> *Premiere:* 5 January 1985, Groningen

Divertimento   1949 (DO)   dur. 12′; instr. 3333-4331 - timp,   **W-159**
perc, str. 5
> 1. Bransle simple (Allegretto); 2. Rigaudon (Allegro
> assai); 3. Rondeau (Allegretto)
> *Commission:* Resident Orchestra of The Hague
> *Premiere:* March 1950

Fanfare de Jeanne d'Arc   1944 (DO)   dur. 7′; instr. 3333-4431 -   **W-160**
timp, perc, arp, str. 5
> *Commission:* Dutch Government

Gedenckclanck: Suite for Orchestra   1938 (UE)   dur. 28′;   **W-161**
instr. 3332-4320 - timp, perc, cel, pf, arp, str. 5
> 1. Intrada: Marcia siciliano; 2. Pavane; 3. Gagliarde;
> 4. Saltarello; 5. Sarabande; 6. Rondeau; 7. Finale
> (thema con variazioni)
> *Dedication and Premiere:* Concertgebouw Orchestra
> (50th anniversary)

Holland Rhapsody   1949 (Ms.)   dur. 4′; instr. 2222-2330 -   **W-162**
timp, perc, cel, arp, str. 5
> *Commission:* Marshall Plan, U.S.

Mars   1957 (DO)   dur. 5′; instr. 2222-4230 - timp, perc, str. 5   **W-163**
> *Commission:* Dutch Radio

Overture 1   *The Tragic*   1937 (UE)   dur. 10′; instr. 3333-4331 -   **W-164**
timp, perc, cel, str. 5
> *Dedication:* Eduard van Beinum

Overture 2   *The Heroic*   1937 (LEU)   dur. 7′; instr. 2222-4220 -   **W-165**
timp, perc, cel, pf, str. 5
(Gijsbrecht van Aemstel)
> *Dedication:* Albert van Dalsum

Overture 3   *The Symphonic Overture*   1942 (DO)   dur. 12′;   **W-166**
instr. 3333-4431 - timp, perc, str. 5

Overture 4   *Symphonic Prologue*   1942 (UE)   dur. 17′; instr.   **W-167**
3333-4431 - timp, perc, str. 5
> *Commission and Dedication:* Vienna Philharmonic
> Orchestra
> *Premiere:* Occasion of the Orchestra's Centennial

Overture 5 *Holland Festival Overture* 1954 (DO) dur. 12'; **W-168**
    instr. 2222-4331 - timp, perc, str. 5
        1. Lento; 2. Allegro con brio
        Award: Price of the Dutch Government
        Commission: Dutch Government
        Dedication: Eduard van Beinum
        Premiere: 18 March 1965

Overture 6 *The Irish* 1961 (DO) dur. 10'; instr. 3232-4331 - **W-169**
    timp, perc, cel, pf, str. 5
        Premiere: 6 May 1961, Dublin, Ireland

Serenade 1953 (DO) dur. 18'; instr. 2222-4331 - timp, perc, **W-170**
    str. 5
        1. Intrada; 2. Marcia giacosa; 3. Romanza;
        4. Scherzo; 5. Finale
        Commission: Dutch Radio
        Premiere: 9 July 1953, Hilversum

Symphonic Scherzo 1953 (DO) dur. 15'; instr. 3333-4331 - **W-171**
    timp, perc, cel, pf, arp, str. 5
        Lento Allegro
        Commission: City of Bremen, Germany
        Premiere: 23 November 1953, Paul von Kempen,
           conductor

Symphonic Variations 1 1936 (UE) dur. 16'; instr. 3333-4431 - **W-172**
    timp, perc, arp, str. 5
        1. Lento; 2. Allegro; 3. Listesso tempo; 4. Con
        moto; 5. Allegro; 6. Adagio; 7. Presto; 8. Meno
        mosso; 9. Allegro vivace; 10. Pesante
        Award: Radio Nederland, Hilversum (1950)
        Dedication: Karl Böhm (in memory)

Symphonic Variations 2 *Ballade, Variations on a Mediaeval* **W-173**
    Theme 1950 (DO) dur. 9'; instr. 2222-4330 - timp,
    perc, arp, str. 5
        Commission: Royal Dutch Music Foundation
           (75th anniversary)
        Dedication: Eduard Flipse

Symphonic Variations 3 *Dance Variations* 1956 (DO) **W-174**
    dur. 18'; instr. 3233-4331 - timp, perc, pf, str. 5

Symphonic Variations 3 (*continued*)
> 1. Gavotte; 2. Menuet; 3. Marcia-Trio-Marcia;
> 4. Sarabande; 5. Cancan; 6. Cancan; 7. Air
> (Boutons); 8. Perpetuum mobile (galop); 9. Blues
> 10. Rumba
> *Commission:* Dutch Radio

Symphonic Variations 4   *Variations on a South-African Theme*   **W-175**
1960 (DO)   dur. 21'; instr. 3333-4431 - timp, perc, cel,
str. 5
> 1. Introduction; 2. Theme; 3. Meno mosso;
> 4. Sarabande; 5. Scherzo; 6. Molto Adagio;
> 7. Finale
> *Commission:* Johan Wagenaar Foundation
> *Premiere:* 14 April 1961, Johannesburg, South
>   Africa

Vier Nederlandse dansen   1957 (DO)   dur. 12'; instr.   **W-176**
2222-4230 - timp, perc, str. 5
> 1. Friese Plof; 2. Hollandse Boerendans; 3. Brabants
> Air; 4. Gelderse Polka
> *Commission:* Dutch Radio

Vijf Nederlandse dansen   1976 (HARM)   dur. 15'; instr.   **W-177**
3231-2220 - timp, perc 3, str. 5
(Five Dutch Dances) Suite 2
> 1. Dans uit Terschelling (Moderato); 2. Westfriese
> dans (Molto allegro); 3. Drentse dans (Scherzo);
> 4. Westfriese dans (Berceux); 5. Rielen
> *Commission:* Harmonia
> *Dedication:* Ru Sevenhuysen

Concertos (Symphony Orchestra)

Concerto for Flute 1   1956 (DO)   dur. 22'; instr. 2121-2110 -   **W-178**
timp, pf, str. 5
> 1. Lento-allegro molto; 2. Scherzo presto;
> 3. Passacaglia-grave; 4. Molto vivace
> *Commission:* "Sempre Crescendo," University of
>   Leiden
> *Dedication:* Jaap Stotijn
> *Premiere:* 8 December 1956

Concerto for Harp 1967 (DO) dur. 20'; instr. 2222-4220 -   **W-179**
    timp, perc 2, cel, str. 5
        1. Lento - Allegro; 2. Grave; 3. Presto
        Dedication: Phia Berghout
        Premiere: September 1967, Resident Orchestra
           of The Hague; Phia Berghout, soloist;
           Willem v. Otterloo, conductor
        (See *Concertos [Wind Orchestra]* - **W-230**)

Concerto for Organ 1 1952 (DO) dur. 24'; instr. 2222-3331 -   **W-180**
    timp, perc, str. 5
        1. Lento allegro; 2. Adagio; 3. Allegro giocoso
        Commission: International Organ Concours, Haarlem
        Premiere: 7 October 1952; Anton Heiller, soloist

Concerto for Organ 2 1966 (DO) dur. 24'; instr. 2222-3320 -   **W-181**
    timp, perc, str. 5
        1. Lento-agitato; 2. Tranquillo; 3. Allegro
        Commission: International Organ Concours, Harlem
        Premiere: 8 July 1966; Anton Heiller, soloist

Concerto for Piano 1 1939 (DO) dur. 30'; instr. 2232-4331 -   **W-182**
    timp, perc, cel, str. 5
        1. Allegro; 2. Adagio; 3. Allegro vivace
        Dedication and Premiere: May 1940, Concertgebouw
           Orchestra; Cor de Groot, soloist

Concerto for Piano 2 *Atlantic Dances* 1955 (DO) dur. 12';   **W-183**
    instr. 1121-1220 - perc, str. 5
        1. Ragtime; 2. Blues; 3. Tango
        Commission: City of Hannover
        Dedication: O. Koebel
        Premiere: 17 October 1955; O. Koebel, soloist

Concerto for Saxophone 1951 (DO) dur. 20'; instr.   **W-184**
    2222-3331 - timp, perc, str. 5
        1. Allegro; 2. Largo; 3. Presto
        Premiere: Oslo, Norway; Jules de Vries, soloist
        (See *Concertos [Wind Orchestra]* - **W-231**)

Concerto for Viola 1965 (DO) dur. 18'; instr. str. 5   **W-185**
        1. Quasi lento-allegro; 2. Adagio; 3. Allegro molto
        Commission: Joke Vermeulen
        Premiere: 12 July 1966, Rotterdam, Dutch Chamber
           Orchestra; Joke Vermeulen, soloist; David
           Zinman, conductor

Concerto for Violin 1   1928 (Ms.)   dur. 20′; instr. 2123-3231 -   **W-186**
    timp, perc, str. 5
        1. Lento moderato — Allegro vivace; 2. Lento;
        3. Allegro moderato

Concerto for Violin 2   1935 (DO)   dur. 22′; instr. 3333-2221 -   **W-187**
    timp, perc, str. 5
        1. Allegro; 2. Molto adagio; 3. Allegro vivace
        Premiere: December 1935, Utrecht

Concerto for Violin 3   1944 (DO)   dur. 30′; instr. 2222-3200 -   **W-188**
    timp, str. 5
        1. Allegro; 2. Largo; 3. Allegro assai
        Dedication: Herman v. d. Vegt
        Premiere: 4 April 1957

Concerto for Violin 4   1947 (DO)   dur. 26′; instr. 3111-2000 -   **W-189**
    timp, str. 5
        1. Allegro; 2. Canzona; 3. Rondo: Allegro vivace
        Commission: Utrecht University Student Orchestra;
            F. Le Coultre, soloist; Hans B. Buys, conductor
        Dedication: Hans B. Buys

Concerto for Violoncello 1   1930 (Ms.)   dur. 15′; instr.   **W-190**
    1111-1110 - perc, str. 5
        1. Allegro moderato-allegro; 2. Largo; 3. Allegro
        ma non troppo
        Dedication: Henk van Wezel
        Premiere: 27 September 1930, Concertgebouw
        Orchestra; Henk van Wezel, soloist

Concerto for Violoncello 2   1939 (DO)   dur. 22′; instr.   **W-191**
    2232-3220 - timp, perc, str. 5
        1. Allegro molto; 2. Largo; 3. Allegro
        Premiere: 29 January 1955, The Hague; Caspar
        Cassado, soloist

Double-Concerto 1 for Two Violins   1954 (DO)   dur. 24′;   **W-192**
    instr. 2222-4331 - timp, perc, pf, str. 5
        1. Pesante; 2. Adagio; 3. Vivace
        Award: Best Composition of the Year (1959) by
        UNESCO
        Commission: Johan Wagenaar Foundation
        Premiere: Resident Orchestra of The Hague;
        Theo Olof and Herman Krebbers, soloists;
        Willem v. Otterloo, conductor

Double-Concerto 3 for Two Pianos   1964 (DO)   dur. 24';   **W-193**
  instr. 3222-3311 - timp, perc, cel, str. 5
    1. Lento-allegro; 2. Lento; 3. Presto
    Award: Premio Marzoto Prize, Venice, Italy (1964)
    Commission: Dutch Government
    Premiere: 24 September 1964, Venice, "Teatro
        Venice"; Lorenzi and Gorino, soloists; M.
        Pradella, conductor

Double-Concerto 4 for Violin and Viola   1965 (DO)   dur. 21';   **W-195**
  instr. 3220-3200 - timp, perc, cel, pf, str. 5
    1. Lento-allegro; 2. Adagio-moderato
    Commission: Dutch Government

Double-Concerto 5 for Two Violins   1969 (DO)   dur. 20';   **W-195**
  instr. 0000-0040 - timp, perc, str. 5
    1. Moderato; 2. Scherzo-presto; 3. Adagio-presto
    Commission: Dutch Government
    Premiere: 25 October 1969, Hilversum, Radio
        Philharmonic Orchestra; Bouw Lemkes and
        Jeanne Vos, soloists; Charles de Wolff, conductor

Fanfare for 4 Trumpets   1944 (DO)   dur. 7'; instr. 3333-4431 -   **W-196**
  timp, perc, arp, str. 5

Quadruple-Concerto for 4 Saxophones   1984 (DO)   dur. 20';   **W-197**
  instr. 2232-4331 - timp, perc 4, str. 5
    1. Introduzione e allegro; 2. Lento; 3. Finale
    Commission: Dutch Fund for the Creative Arts
    Dedication: Brabants Saxophone Quartet
    (See *Concertos [Wind Orchestra]* - **W-236**)

Triple-Concerto 1 for Violin, Violoncello and Piano   1942 (DO)   **W-198**
  dur. 20'   instr. 3232-3110 - timp, perc, cel, str. 5
    1. Allegro; 2. Lento; 3. Allegretto
    Commission: Dutch Radio
    Premiere: October 1942, Concertgebouw Orchestra;
        W. Noske, A. Loerkens, Theo v. d. Pas, soloists;
        Toon Verhey, conductor

Triple-Concerto 3 for Flute, Oboe and Clarinet   1981 (DO)   **W-199**
  dur. 32'; instr. 0013-4431 - timp, perc, str. 5
    1. Introduction and allegro energico; 2. Cadence
    accompagnate; 3. Finale

Triple-Concerto 3 for Flute, Oboe and Clarinet - (*continued*)
  Commission: City of Eindhoven, Netherlands
  Premiere: 20 May 1985, s'Hertogenbosch, Brabants
    Orchestra
  (See *Concertos [Wind Orchestra]* - **W-238**)

Wind Orchestra

Ariosi e Fugati 1979 (MO)   dur. 11'; instr. 0000-4 sax (satb) -   **W-200**
  4,2 + 3 bugle + 3 cornet, 3 + 3 euph + 2, bar,2 - timp, perc
  for fanfare orchestra
      1. Andante; 2. Allegro; 3. Largo; 4. Allegro
  Commission: Dutch Fund for the Creative Arts
  Dedication: J. P. Laro

Armageddon 1968 (P)   dur. 14'; instr. 1 + pic + alto fl + bass   **W-201**
  fl,1 + oboe d'am + cor ingl + hph, 1 + bass cl + 2 c. bass
  cl,2 + 2 c. fag - 6642 - timp, perc 5, cel, pf, soprano or ondes
  martinot   with soprano and tape (2 sound tracks)
      1. Tape Solo; 2. Moderato with Orchestra - Tutti;
      3. Tape Solo; 4. Lento for Woodwinds; 5. Episode
      for Percussion, Soprano and Tape; 6. Chorale for
      Brass, with Woodwind and Percussion; 7. Finale
      for Soprano, Orchestra and Tape (Dies irae)
  Commission and Dedication: Robert Boudreau
  Premiere: 27 June 1968, Pittsburgh, U.S.;
      American Wind Symphony Orchestra

Ciacona concertante 1978 (Ms.)   dur. 10'; instr. wind   **W-202**
  orchestra

Ciacona seria 1982 (B&H)   dur. 12'; instr. 0000-2 + solo,2 + 2   **W-203**
  bugles + cornet + flugelhorn, 2 bar, 2 euph, 2 tuba - timp,
  perc 3 (brass band)
  Commission: Boosey and Hawkes

Ciacona seria 1985 (B&H)   dur. 12'; instr. 0000 - 6 sax   **W-204**
  (2s2atb) - 4,2 + 3 bugle + 3 cornet, 3 + 2 euph,2 - timp, perc 3
  (Verses for Fanfare Orchestra)
  Eight variations

Epiphany 1979 (MO)   dur. 13'; instr. 2 + pic,1,3 + E♭ cl + alto   **W-205**
cl + bass cl,1 - 4 sax (2atb) - 4,3,3 + euph,2 timp, perc 2
(I tre re)
>1. Allegro; 2. Listesso tempo I; 3. Piu mosso;
>4. Listesso tempo I; 5. Moderato; 6. Grave;
>7. Presto; 8. Piu animato; 9. Ad lib piu animato
>*Commission:* Music Festival, Uster, Switzerland
>*Dedication:* Jean Claessens
>*Premiere:* August 1979, Kerkelijek Harmonie
>   Thorn, Walter Boeyken, conductor

Figures sonores 1984 (MO)   dur. 11'; instr. 2 + pic,2 + eh,   **W-206**
3(div) + E♭ cl + alto cl + bass cl,0 - 4 sax (2atb) - 4,3 + 3
cornet,4 + 2 euph,1 - timp, perc 4, cb
>1. Quasi moderato; 2. Quasi allegro molto;
>3. Grave pesante e severo
>*Commission:* Dutch Fund for the Creative Arts
>*Dedication:* Jean Claessens
>*Premiere:* 9 December 1984, Koninlijke Harmonie
>   Thorn, Jan Cober, conductor

Golden Age 1979 (MO)   dur. 14'; instr. 2 + pic,2,3 + E♭   **W-207**
cl + bass cl,2 - 4 sax (2atb) - 4,2 + 3 cornet,3 + euph,2 - timp,
perc 3, cb
>1. Haagse praal (intrada pomposo); 2. Gelderse
>galjaard; 3. Friese mars; 4. Zeeuwse jig en parade
>finale
>*Commission:* SONMO (Holland)

Greensleeves 1970 (P)   dur. 7'; instr. 1 + pic + alto fl,2 + eh,   **W-208**
1 + E♭ cl + bass cl,2 + c. fag - 4431 - timp, perc 4, arp, cel
>*Commission:* American Wind Symphony Orchestra,
>   Robert Boudreau, conductor
>*Dedication:* Irma d'Ascenzio

Images 1983 (MO)   dur. 14'; instr. 0000 - 6 sax (2s2atb) -   **W-209**
4,2 + 2 cornet,3 + euph,2 - timp, perc 3, cb   for fanfare
orchestra
>1. Energico; 2. Notturno; 3. Giocoso
>*Premiere:* 29 January 1984, Someren, Wind
>   Orchestra of St. Joseph, Alex Schillings,
>   conductor

Intrada 1942 (DO)   dur. 7'; instr. 2160 - 3 sax - 6436 -   **W-210**
timp, perc, cb

Introduction, Variations and Indonesian National Anthem   **W-211**
    1986 (Ms.)   dur. 6'; instr. 2 + pic,2,3 + bass cl,3 - 4441 -
    timp, perc 4, arp
        Commission: American Wind Symphony Orchestra,
        Robert Boudreau, conductor
        Premiere: August 1986, New York

Lieshout en zijn molens   1976 (DO)   dur. 15'; instr. 2 + pic,2,4   **W-212**
    E♭ cl + bass cl,2 - 4 sax (2atb) - 4,2(div) + 3 cornet,3 + euph,2
    - timp, perc 3   for fanfare orchestra
(The Windmills of Lieshout)
        1. Overture; 2. Scherzo; 3. Notturno; 4. Rondo
        Commission: Dutch Government
        Premiere: 21 August 1976, Centennial of Lieshout
        Wind Orchestra

Old Dutch Christmas Carol   1970 (P)   dur. 4'; instr.   **W-213**
    0000-4441 - tape, arp, cel, glock, perc 3
        Commission: American Wind Symphony Orchestra,
        Robert Boudreau, conductor

Partita bucolica   1960 (DO)   dur. 20'; instr. 1,1,3 + E♭ cl,1 -   **W-214**
    3 sax (atb) - 4,2 + 2 cornet,3 + 2 euph,2 - timp, perc 3, cb
        1. Intrada seria; 2. Segnale; 3. Ballade; 4. Scherzo
        5. Canzonetta malinconica; 6. Finale
        Commission: Dutch Radio

Pittsburgh Concerto   1965 (P)   dur. 18'; instr. 0010-2220 -   **W-215**
    timp, perc, pf, cel, tape (2 tracks)
        1. Toccata; 2. Nocturne; 3. Finale
        Commission: American Wind Symphony Orchestra,
        Robert Boudreau, conductor
        Dedication: Robert Boudreau
        Premiere: 10 July 1965

Ragtime   1969 (P)   dur. 6'; instr. Group I: 0000 - 1340 - timp   **W-216**
    Group II: 0000 - 4211 - timp, perc
        1. Allegro
        Commission: American Wind Symphony Orchestra,
        Robert Boudreau
        Premiere: 1969

Reflections   1980 (MO)   dur. 15′; instr. 2 + pic,2,3 + E♭   **W-217**
cl + alto cl + bass cl,2 - 4 sax (2 atb) - 4,2 + 2 cornet,3 + 2
euph,1 - timp, perc 4, cel, cb
>   1. Impressions; 2. Interplay; 3. Evolutions
>   *Commission:* American Bandmasters Association
>   *Dedication:* Arnald Gabriel
>   *Premiere:* June 1981, U.S. Air Force Band, Arnald
>   Gabriel, conductor

Royal Fanfare   1981 (Ms.)   dur 4′; instr. 0000 - 5552 - timp 2, perc   **W-218**
>   *Commission:* American Wind Symphony Orchestra
>   (25th anniversary)

Sagas   1984 (Ms.)   dur. 20′; instr. 0040 - 6 sax (2s2atb) -   **W-219**
4,4,4 + 3 euph,2 - timp, per 3
>   1. Het spoken driesken (The Trio of Ghosts); 2. In
>   memoriam; 3. De vuurmannen (Fireman)
>   *Commission:* Dutch Fund for the Creative Arts
>   *Premiere:* 1985, World Music Competition; Leon
>   Adams, conductor

Sinfonietta 2   1981 (MO)   dur. 15′; instr. 2 + pic,2,3(div) + E♭   **W-220**
cl + bass cl,1 - 4 sax (2 atb) - 4,3,3 + 2 euph,2 - timp, perc 3, cb
>   1. Proemiale; 2. Moto martellato; 3. Canto
>   polimelodico; 4. Finale scherzando
>   *Commission:* Dutch Government
>   *Dedication:* Jean Claessens
>   *Premiere:* 1982, Koninklijke Harmonie Societeit
>   Asterius, Oisterwijk

Symphony 13   1966 (P)   dur. 15′; instr. 3 + pic + alto fl,2 + eh,   **W-221**
3 + bass cl,3 + c, fag - 5551 - timp, perc 3, pf, cel
>   1. Lento; 2. Allegro moderato; 3. Lento allegro
>   *Commission:* American Wind Symphony Orchestra,
>   Robert Boudreau, conductor
>   *Dedication:* Robert Boudreau
>   *Premiere:* 29 June 1967, Pittsburgh, U.S.

Symphony 15 *Conflicts and Confluences* 1983 (MO)   dur. 15′;   **W-222**
instr. 2 + pic,2,3 + E♭ cl + alto cl + bass cl,2 - 4 sax (2atb) -
2 + 3 cornet,4 + 2 euph,4 - timp, perc 3
>   1. Allegro; 2. Adagio molto; 3. Scherzo finale
>   *Commission:* Dutch Fund for the Creative Arts
>   *Premiere:* Maastrichts Conservatory Wind Orchestra,
>   Sef Pijpers, conductor

Three Apparitions of a Hymn   1984 (P)   dur. 15'; instr.   W-223
    4 + pic,3 + eh,4 + bass cl,2 + c. fag - 4541 - timp, perc 3,
    cel, arp, sopr. choir (Unison) organ, tape
        1. Molto moderato; 2. Largo; 3. Allegro moderato
        (Fugue)
        Commission: American Wind Symphony Orchestra,
            Robert Boudreau, conductor
        Premiere: June 1984, U.S.

Tower Music   1969 (P)   dur. 16'; instr. Group I: 0000 - 4211 -   W-224
    timp, perc 2, tape; Group II: 0000 - 1340 - timp
        1. Intrada; 2. Slagwerk Solo; 3. Passacaglia
        Commission: American Wind Symphony Orchestra,
            Robert Boudreau, conductor
        Premiere: 13 July 1969

Transitions   1972 (SP)   dur. 14'; instr. 2 + pic,2 + eh,3(div) + Eb   W-225
    cl + alto cl + bass cl,2 - 4 sax (2atb) - 4,3 + 3 cornet,4 + 2
    euph,1 - timp 2, perc 4, cb
        Commission: College Band Directors National
            Association
        Premiere: 13 January 1973, University of Illinois
            Symphonic Band, Harry Begian, conductor

Concertos (Wind Orchestra)

Concerto for Clarinet   1979 (P)   dur. 16'; instr. 2 + alto   W-226
    fl + bass fl,2 + eh + hph, bass cl + c. bass cl, 2 + c. fag -
    4431 - timp, perc 4, pf
        1. Moderato (Arabesque over Crossreading
        Harmonies); 2. Slow (Lines and Lyrics); 3. Quick
        (Rhythms and Ratios)
        Commission: Robert Boudreau for International
            Clarinet Competition
        Dedication: American Wind Symphony Orchestra,
            Robert Boudreau, conductor
        Premiere: 11 May 1979, U.S.

Concert Piece for Clarinet   *Phantasy and Quodlibet on*   W-227
    Marksmenmarch-Motifs   1980 (P)   dur. 5'; instr. 2 + alto
    fl + bass fl,2 + eh + hph, bass cl + c. bass cl, 2 + 2 c. fag -
    4000 - timp

Concerto for English Horn *American Folksong Suite* 1975 (P)   **W-228**
    dur. 22'; instr. 3 + pic,2(ob d'am) + hph,3 + bass cl,2 + c. fag
    - 4331 - timp, perc 3, arp
        1. Ballad of the Wayfaring Stranger; 2. Scherzo
        Metamorphosis of the Wayfaring Stranger;
        3. Variations on the Blue-Tail Fly; 4. Quodlibet -
        "Nobody Knows the Trouble"
        Commission: American Wind Symphony Orchesta,
           Robert Boudreau, conductor
        Dedication: Robert Boudreau
        Premiere: 11 May 1976, U.S.

Concerto for Flute 2   1963 (P)   dur. 12'; instr. 3333-4431 -   **W-229**
    timp, perc 3
        1. Allegro; 2. Adagio; 3. Vivace
        Commission: American Wind Symphony Orchestra,
           Robert Boudreau, conductor
        Dedication: Walter Hinrichsen
        Premiere: 27 June 1963, New York; Jean Pierre
           Rampal, soloist

Concerto for Harp   1967 (P)   dur. 20'; instr. 1 + pic + alto   **W-230**
    fl + bass fl,1 + ob d'am + eh + hph, 1 + bassethorn + bass
    cl + c. bass cl,2 + 2 c. fag - 4431 - timp, perc 4, cel
        1. Lento - Allegro; 2. Grave; 3. Presto
        Commission: American Wind Symphony Orchestra,
           Robert Boudreau, conductor
        Dedication: Phia Berghout
        Premiere: June 1967, American Wind Symphony
           Orchestra, Marcela Kozikova, soloist; Robert
           Boudreau, conductor
        (See *Concertos [Symphony Orchestra]* - **W-179**)

Concerto for Saxophone   1951 (DO)   dur. 20'; instr.   **W-231**
    2 + pic,2,4 + 2Eb cl + bass cl,2(c. fag) - 2 sax (tb) - 4,3 + 2
    cornet + 2 bugle,4 + 4 bar,2 - timp, perc 2, cb
        1. Allegro; 2. Largo (notturno); 3. Presto (rondo)
        Premiere: 3 August 1951, The Hague, Royal
           Military Band, Rocus van Yperen, conductor
        (See *Concertos [Symphony Orchestra]* - **W-184**)

Concerto for Trombone   1986 (P)   dur. 12'; instr. 4,3,4 + bass   **W-232**
    cl,0 - 4441 - timp, perc 4
        1. Grave; 2. Doppio movimento; 3. Poco meno;
        4. A tempo; 5. Coda (with cadenza)

Concerto for Trombone - (*continued*)
>   *Commission:* American Wind Symphony Orchestra,
>   Don Lucas, soloist; Robert Boudreau, conductor
>   *Premiere:* 24 May 1987, U.S.

Concerto for Violoncello 3   1985 (P)   dur. 16' instr. 4(pic),   W-233
2,3 + bass cl,0 - 4441 - timp, perc 3
>   1. Contrasti; 2. Arioso; 3. Giocoso
>   *Commission:* American Wind Symphony Orchestra,
>   Robert Boudreau, conductor
>   *Premiere:* July 1986, American Wind Symphony
>   Orchestra, Anne Martindale Williams; Robert
>   Boudreau, conductor

Double-Concerto 2 for Bassoon and Contra-Bassoon   1964 (P)   W-234
dur. 16'; instr. 3 + pic + alto fl,2,2 + bass cl,0 - 3331 -
timp, perc
>   1. Lento; 2. Allegro; 3. Lento; 4. Allegro
>   *Commission:* American Wind Symphony Orchestra,
>   Robert Boudreau, conductor
>   *Dedication:* Paul Hindemith (in remembrance)
>   *Premiere:* 1964, American Wind Symphony Orchestra

Harpsichord Concerto in A of J. S. Bach   1986 (P)   dur. 15';   W-235
instr. 2 + alto fl,2 + 2 cor ingl,0,4 - 03(ad lib)00 + basso continuo
(Transcription of BWV 1055)
>   1. Allegro; 2. Larghetto; 3. Allegro ma non tanto
>   *Commission:* American Wind Symphony Orchestra,
>   Robert Boudreau, conductor

Quadruple-Concerto for Four Saxophones   1984 (DO)   dur. 20';   W-236
instr. 2 + pic,1,3,1 - 4 sax (2atb) - 4,2 + 2 cornet,3 + 3 euph,2 -
timp, perc 3, cb
>   1. Introduzione e allegro; 2. Lento; 3. Finale
>   *Commission:* Dutch Fund for the Creative Arts
>   *Dedication:* Brabants Saxophone Quartet
>   *Premiere:* 19 December 1984, Tilburg; Brabants
>   Saxophone Quartet, soloists; Walter Boeykens,
>   conductor
>   (See *Concertos [Symphony Orchestra]* - **W-197**)

Triple-Concerto 2 for Three French Horns   1970 (P)   dur. 15';   W-237
instr. 3(pic),3,3,3 - 0441 - tape, timp, perc 5, cel
>   1. Marche royale; 2. Nocturne; 3. Finale joyeux

Commission: American Wind Symphony Orchestra,
   Robert Boudreau, conductor
Premiere: 26 August 1970, West Harvord, U.S.

Triple-Concerto 3 for Flute, Oboe and Clarinet 1981 (DO)   **W-238**
   dur. 15'; instr. 3,2,3 + bass cl,3 - 4 sax (2 atb) - 4,4,3 + 2
   euph,1 - timp, perc 3, cb
         1. Introduzione e allegro energico; 2. Cadenze
         accompagnate; 3. Finale
         (See *Concertos [Symphony Orchestra]* - **W-199**)

Accordion Orchestra

Twentse suite 1976 (DO)   dur. 10'; instr. ad lib soloists   **W-239**
   (woodwind, brass or accordion) and four groups of
   accordions
         1. Intrada; 2. Air; 3. Scherzo; 4. Finale
         Commission: City of Hengelo, Netherlands
         Premiere: 21 May 1976, Hengelo

5 CHORAL WORKS

Mixed Choir with Symphony Orchestra

Apocalypse 1948 (DO) dur. 100' oratorio for solo voices   **W-240**
   (SATB) and mixed choir; instr. 3333-4431 - timp, perc 3,
   cel, arp, pf, str. 5
Text: Dutch (Bible)
         1. Proloog (Prologue); 2. Het openen van den
         hemel (The Opening of the Heaven); 3. Het
         openen van het boek der 7 zegelen (The Opening
         of the Book of 7 Seals); 4. De Rampen op aarde

Apocalypse - (*continued*)
(The Catastrophes on Earth); 5. Het oordeel (The
Last Judgement); 6. De Godsstad (The City of
God); 7. Epiloog (Epilogue)
Commission: City of Rotterdam
Premiere: 25 November 1949, Rotterdam
Philharmonic Orchestra; Otto Glastra van
Loon, conductor

Cantata 1 *Festival Cantata* 1936 (Ms.) dur. 25' for four   **W-241**
soli, mixed choir, and children's choir; instr. 3333-6632
- timp, perc 3, cel, arp, org, str. 5
Text: Dutch (Werumeus Buning)
1. Introduction; 2. Chorale; 3. Quartet; 4. Soprano
aria; 5. Bass aria; 6. Soprano aria; 7. Siciliano
(children's choir); 8. Male chorus; 9. Tenor aria;
10. Finale
Commission: Dutch Radio (on the occasion of the
wedding of Princess Juliana)

Cantata 2 *Honestum petimus usque* 1937 (DO) dur. 23'   **W-242**
for soprano and chamber choir; instr. 2030-2110 - timp,
perc, cel, pf, str. 5
Text: Dutch (Albert Verwey)
1. Lento allegro; 2. Adagio; 3. Allegretto;
4. Recitativo; 5. Finale
Commission: Amsterdam Student Corps
Premiere: 28 June 1937, W. V. Warmelo, conductor

Cantata 3 1954 (Ms.)
(See *Mixed Choir with Wind Orchestra* - **W-254**)

Cantata 4 1954 (DO) dur. 12' for mixed choir; instr.   **W-243**
2222-4331 - timp, perc, str. 5
Text: Dutch (anon.)
3 old folksongs
1. Introduction; 2. Waer dat men sich al keert of
wendt (Where Everybody Turns to); 3. Tussenspel
(Interlude); 4. Hoe groot, O Heer (How Great, O
Lord); 5. Merck tochhoe sterck (Perceive How
Strong); 6. Fuga
Commission: Dutch Radio
Premiere: 30 April 1954

Cantata 5 *Laus pacis* 1956 (DO)
(See *Male Choir with Wind Orchestra* - **W-355**)

Cantata 6 *Laus stulititiae* 1961 (DO) dur. 25' for mixed   **W-244**
choir and 4 wind instruments obligato, 4 wind instruments;
ad lib, perc, pf, violin, viola, vlc, cb
(Praise of Folly)
Text: Latin (Erasmus)
      1. Inscriptio (Inscription); 2. Stultitia loquitur
      (Folly Speaks); 3. Stultitia mulieris (Folly of
      Women); 4. Stultitia viri (Folly of Man); 5. Stultitia
      deorum (Folly of the Gods); 6. Stultitia cupidinis
      (Folly of the Greed); 7. Stultitia civitatis (Folly of
      the State); 8. Epilogus stultitia (Epilogue to Folly)
      Commission: Dutch Government
      Dedication: Norman Demuth
      Premiere: 1961, Utrecht Orchestra

Cantata 7 *Ballade van de bloeddorstige jagter* 1970 (Ms.)   **W-245**
dur. 25' for prerecorded soli and mixed choir; instr.
3333-4431 - timp, perc, pf, arp, cel, str. 5, tape
(Ballad of the Bloodthirsty Hunter)
Text: South African (G. Watermeyer)
      Award: Prix Italia (1971)
      Commission: South African Radio
      Premiere: 22 November 1970, Johannesburg,
          South Africa; Anton Hartman, conductor

Cantata 8 *Song of Myself* 1973 (P)
(See *Mixed Choir with Wind Orchestra* - **W-255**)

Cantata 9 *Christiaan Huygens Cantata* 1987 (Ms.) dur. 15' for   **W-246**
soprano and tenor solo, mixed choir; instr. 1111-0100 - str. 5
Text: Dutch (Constantijn Huygens and Henk Badings)
      1. Scheepspraet (Speaking on a Ship); 2. Op de
      dood van Sterre (The Death of My Wife Sterre);
      3. Ostinato - Aen mijnen soon (To My Son); 4. De
      geleerden zijn blind (The Scientists Are Blind);
      5. Danssen; 6. Koraal: Nae leven (After Life);
      7. Finale: Christian Huygens was een groot man
      (Christian Huygens Was a Great Man)
      Commission: Leo Bonebakker
      (Orchestral Suite is published by HARM; see
          Chamber Orchestra)

Een kindelijn zo lovelijk 1967 (Ms.) dur. 2'; instr. 1111-1100 -   **W-247**
perc, str. 5
(A Child So Lovely)
Text: Dutch (anon.)

Heer Jezus heeft een hofken   1967 (Ms.)   dur. 3'   for soprano   **W-248**
and mixed choir; instr. 1111-1100 - perc, str. 5
(The Lord Has a Small House)
Text: Dutch (anon.)

Hier is onze fiere pinksterbloem   1967 (Ms.)   dur. 2'   for   **W-249**
soprano, baritone and mixed choir; instr. 1111-1100 - perc,
str. 5
(Here Is Our Proud Spring Flower)
Text: Dutch (anon.)

Jonah   1963 (DO)   dur. 30'   oratorio for 3 solo voices (TTB)   **W-250**
mixed choir, male choir and electronic music; instr.
6130-2220 - timp, perc, pf, cel, str. 5
(stereo - radiophonic sound poem)
Text: English (Bible)
> 1. Prologue; 2. Storm Episode; 3. First Prayer of
> Jonah; 4. Conversion of Ninevah; 5. Tenor Aria;
> 6. Second Prayer of Jonah; 7. Miracle Tree
> Episode; 8. Finale; 9. Epilogue
> *Commission:* Dutch Radio
> *Dedication:* Dutch Consul in Adelaide, Australia,
>   Eric McLaughlin
> *Premiere:* 3 June 1962, Adelaide, Australia

Klaagsang   1970 (DO)   dur. 12'   for mixed choir; instr.   **W-251**
2222-3330 - timp, perc 2, cel, pf, str. 5
(Lament Song)
Text: South African (N. P. van Wijk Louw)
> *Dedication:* Rosa and Gladstone Louw
> *Premiere:* 31 May 1971, Capetown, South Africa

Psalm 147   1959 (DO)   dur. 30'   for childrens choir and   **W-252**
mixed choir; instr. 3232-4331 - timp, perc 3, cel, pf, str. 5
Text: Latin (Bible)
> 1. Introduction - Choral Fugato; 2. Choral Canon;
> 3. Motet; 4. Choral; 5. Intermezzo; 6. Recitative;
> 7. Chorale; 8. Choral Fugue
> *Commission:* Dutch Radio
> *Premiere:* 20 November 1959, Amsterdam

Die winter is vergangen   1967 (Ms.)   dur. 2'; instr. 1111-1100 -   **W-253**
perc, str. 5
(The Winter Is Over)
Text: Dutch (anon.)

Mixed Choir with Wind Orchestra

Cantata 3   1954 (Ms.)   dur. 35'   for mixed choir, female choir,   **W-254**
male choir, children's choir; instr. 2 + pic,2,3(div) + 2 E♭
cl + bass cl,2 + c. fag - 3 sax(atb) - 4,3 + 2 bugle + 3 cornet,
4 + 2 bar + 2 bar + 2 euph,2 - timp, org, carillon, cb
Text: Dutch (C. Rijnsdorp and Henk Badings)
   1. Overture; 2. Recitative; 3. Chorale; 4. Elegia;
   5. Intermezzo; 6. Scherzo; 7. Chorale; 8. Recitative
   9. Carillon; 10. Chorale
   Commission: Dutch Radio
   Premiere: 7 June 1954

Cantata 8   *Song of Myself*   1973 (P)   dur. 28'   for narrator   **W-255**
and mixed choir; instr. 4(pic),2,3 + bass cl,2 - 4,4,3,1 -
timp, perc 4, org, tape (ad lib)
Text: English (Walt Whitman)
   1. Stanza 17; 2. Stanza 21; 3. Stanza 17; 4. Stanza 16;
   5. Stanza 17
   Commission: American Wind Symphony Orchestra,
   Robert Boudreau, conductor

Mixed Choir with a Few Instruments

Drei Schwärmereien   1964 (DO)   dur. 12'30''   three songs   **W-256**
for mixed choir and 2 electronic sound tracks
Text: German/English (Lucebert)
   1. Das bisschen Wirklichkeit (A Little Reality);
   2. The Tobacco Frames the Lips; 3. Der Tau
   läutet die Blumen ein (The Dew Upon the Flower);
   Premiere: 24 June 1966, Schorndorf, Germany,
   Schorndorfer Choir, M. Reischle, conductor

Maria   1947 (DO)   dur. 36'   fourteen songs for soli, chamber   **W-257**
choir, fl and vlc
Text: German
   1. Anrufung (Appeal) - R. Paulsen; 2. Sei Gegrüsst
   (Be Welcomed) - F. W. Weber; 3. Des Herren
   Magd (The Master's Servant) - A. Oelerich; 4. Mit
   dem Blumenstrauss (With a Bunch of Flowers) -
   O. zur Linde; 5. Ich sehe dich (I See You) - Novalis

6. Marienlied (Mary's Song) - A. Oelerich; 7. Advent -
A. Althaus; 8. Der Stern (The Star) - H. F.
Christians; 9. Wiegenlied (Lullaby) - A. Oelerich;
10. Auf der Flucht (During the Flight) - H.
Rothhardt; 11. Vor der Passion (Before the
Passion) - R. M. Rilke; 12. Pieta - R. M. Rilke;
13. Maria Himmelfahrt (Mary's Ascension) - M.
von Schenkendorf; 14. O schmerzensreiche Mutter
(O Dolorous Mother) - A. Lorenz
(At the instigation of Felix de Nobel)
Premiere: 1947, Amsterdam, Netherlands Chamber
    Choir, Felix de Nobel, conductor

Three Hymns   1953 (Ms.)   for unison choir and 0000-4332 -   W-258
    timp, org
From Dutch Evangelical Hymnbook (1938)
    Commission: Dutch Radio

Three Psalms   1953 (Ms.)   for unison choir and 0000-4332 -   W-259
    timp, org
        1. Psalm 72; 2. Psalm 100; 3. Psalm 145
        Commission: Dutch Radio

Trois Chansons bretonnes   1946 (BA)   dur. 8'   for mixed   W-260
    choir and pf
Text: French (Th. Botrel)
(Three Breton Songs)
        1. La Nuit en mer (Night at Sea); 2. La Complainte
        des âmes (The Complaint of the Souls); 3. Soir
        d'été (Summer Evening)
        Dedication: Felix de Nobel

Mixed Choir Unaccompanied

Ain boer wol noar zien noaber tou   1979 (KCZB)   dur. 3'30''   W-261
    SATB
(A Farmer Wants to Go to His Neighbor)
Text: Dutch (anon.)
        Commission: Association for the Good of European
            Choirs

Alle dinghe sijn mi te inghi   1928 (Ms.)   dur. 3'   SATB   W-262
(All Things Are Wonderful to Me)
Text: Dutch (Hadewich)

An den Mond   1987 (HARM)   dur. 4'   for alto solo and   W-263
   SSATB
(To the Moon)
Text: German (Johann Wolfgang von Goethe)
      Dedication: Pieter van Moergastel and Lia Ligthart
      Premiere: 2 October 1987, Tilburg, Netherlands,
         Brabant Badings Festival, Kamerkoor Ad
         Parnassum, conducted by Pieter van Moergastel,
         Lia Ligthart, soloist

Aus tiefer Not schrei ich zu Dir   1978 (CSP vol. 1 - HARM)   W-264
   dur. 6'   SATTBB
(I Cry to You Out of Deepest Need)
Text: German (Martin Luther)

Ave maris stella   1987 (CSP vol. 7 - HARM)   dur. 3'   SATB   W-265
(hymn)
Text: Latin

Ballade van de omkransde boot   1987 (CSP vol. 7 - HARM)   W-266
   dur. 4'30''   SATB
(Ballad of the Flowered Boat)
Text: Dutch (Tung-Lin-Fan)

Canamus amici   1957 (HARM)   dur. 3'30''   SATB   W-267
(Friends Let Us Sing)
Text: Dutch (Henk Badings); Latin (M. A. Schwartz)
      (See *Female Choir*)

Cinq Poèmes chinois   1973 (HARM)   dur. 11'   SSAATTBB   W-268
(Five Chinese Poems)
Text: French
         1. Le Destin de l'homme (The Destiny of Man) -
         Kong-Fou-Tsé; 2. Evocation - Tou-Fou; 3. Le
         Pavillon de porcelaine (The China Pavillon) -
         Li-Tai-Po; 4. La Mort (Death) - Lo-Tchan-Nai;
         5. La Danse des dieux (The Dance of the Gods) -
         Li-Tai-Po
      Commission: Cork Festival
      Premiere: 3 May 1973, Cork Festival, Ireland,
         Netherlands Vocal Ensemble, Marinus Voorberg,
         conductor

Claghen   1930 (Ms.)   dur. 1′   SATB   W-269
(Lament)
Text: Dutch (Leopold)

Contrasten   1952 (DO)   dur. 10′   written in the 31-tone system   W-270
Text: Dutch (Hans de Vries)
  1. Serenade - SATB (also published by HARM); 2.
  Elegie - SATB; 3. Soldatenlied (Soldier's Song) -
  TBB (also published by HARM under the title
  "Marslied"); 4. Schertslied (Satirical Song) - SAA;
  5. Geestelijk lied (Sacred Song) - SATB
  Premiere: 1963, Haarlem (Teylers Museum), Quintet
    "Gesualdo da Venosa," Frans Müller, conductor

Doodsbericht   1930 (Ms.)   SATB   W-271
(Obituary)
Text: Dutch (anon.)

Een oudt liedeken   1987 (CSP vol. 7 - HARM)   dur. 1′15″   W-272
  SATB
(Little Old Song)
Text: Dutch (Victor de la Montagne)

Evocations   1962 (HARM)   dur. 8′   SATB   W-273
Text: Dutch (Henk Badings)
  1. Andante; 2. Rubato; 3. Allegro
  Commission: Cork Festival, Ireland

Finnigan's Wake   1978 (CSP vol. 1 - HARM)   dur. 5′   SATB   W-274
Text: English (Irish-American vaudeville, ca. 1870)

Fisches Nachtgesang   1978 (CSP vol. 1 - HARM)   dur. 2′30″   W-275
  SATB/SATB
(Fish's Evening Song)
Text: German (Christian Morgenstern)

Had ick vloghelen als een arend grijs   1933 (Ms.)   dur. 2′30″   W-276
  SATB
(If I Had Wings as a Grey Eagle)
Text: Dutch (anon.)

Herr Jesu deine Angst und Pein   1978 (CSP vol. 1 - HARM)   W-277
  dur. 3′   SATB
(Lord Jesus, Your Fear and Pain)
Text: German (*Evangelisches Kirchengesangbuch* no. 69)

Huwelijkslied 1961 (Ms.) dur. 3' SATB with organ ad lib W-278
(Song of Marriage)
Text: Dutch (Ad. den Besten)
Commission: Dutch Radio

Ick sagh mijn nimphe 1985 (HARM) dur. 2'30'' SATB W-279
(I Saw My Nymph)
Text: Dutch (Jan van der Noot)
Dedication: Jo and Hans Zijderlaan
Premiere: 26 January 1986, Voorburgs, Netherlands
Youth Choir, Ad de Groot, conductor

Ik weet nu zet uw schone deemoed in 1930 (Ms.) dur. 1' W-280
ST (Canon)
(Now I Know It, Start Your Beautiful Humility)
Text: Dutch (P. C. Boutens)

In dir ist Freude 1979 (HARM) dur. 1'40'' SAB W-281
(In Thee Is Joy)
Text: German (*Würthembergischen Choralbuch*)

Java en poèmes (Six Images) 1940 (HARM) dur. 16' SATB W-282
(Java in Poetry)
Text: French (Alla Baud)
1. Ode "La Terre de Java" (O, the Land of Java);
2. Episode "La Brume de Java" (The Fog of Java);
3. Recitatief "Bandjir"; 4. Air "Salak"; 5. Rondeau
"Mes Roses à Java" (My Java Roses); 6. Final,
"Fougères arborescentes" (Tree Ferns)
Award: Radio Diffusion Francaise, Paris (1951)
Premiere: 1 September 1952, Paris, France, Marcel
Couraud, conductor

Kleine Ode für Jan Ter Wey 1976 (Ms.) SATB W-283

Languentibus in purgatorio 1959 (DO) dur. 6' W-284
three performance options:
(Languishing in Purgatory)
Text: Latin (anon.)
1. mixed choir; 2. soloists SATTB; 3. TTB,
soprano solo, alto solo
Commission: by the Vatican for "Lourdiana"
Dedication: To the Holy Father Pope John XXIII
(See *Male Choir Unaccompanied* - **W-284a**)

Lied op het ontzet van Leiden   1979 (Ms.)   dur. 2'   SATB   **W-285**
> or TTBB
(Song of the Liberation of Leiden)
Text: Dutch
>   *Dedication:* European Youth Music Festival,
>   Neerpelt, Belgium

Merck toch hoe sterck   1978 (CSP vol. 1 - HARM)   dur. 3'   **W-286**
> SATB
(Perceive how strong . . .)
Text: Dutch (Valerius Ghedenckclanck)

Missa Antiphonica   1985 (HARM and DO)   dur. 25'   **W-287**
> SATB/SATB
Text: Latin
>   1. Kyrie; 2. Gloria; 3. Sanctus; 4. Benedictus;
>   5. Agnus Dei
>   *Award:* Best European Choral Composition (1988),
>   Berlin
>   *Premiere:* Arnhem, Kleinkoor Toonkunst of
>   Rotterdam, Jan Eelkema, conductor

Missa brevis   1946 (BA)   dur. 15'   SATB   **W-288**
Text: Latin
>   1. Kyrie; 2. Gloria; 3. Credo; 4. Sanctus;
>   5. Benedictus; 6. Agnus Dei

Nieuwjaarscanon   1977 (Ms.)   **W-289**
(An Endless Canon for the New Year)

Notturno triste alla luna   1978 (CSP vol. 1 - HARM)   dur. 4'   **W-290**
> SATB
(Sad Nocturne to the Moon)
Text: Italian (Giacomo Leopardi)

O Mistress Mine   1987 (CSP vol. 7 - HARM)   dur. 1'30'   **W-291**
> SATB
Text: English (William Shakespeare)

Oneindige canon   1960 (Ms.)   Unison   **W-292**
(An Endless Canon of Good Wishes)
Text: Dutch

Oude Ballade   1979 (HARM)   dur. 2'   SAB   **W-293**
Text: Dutch and German (anon.)

Psalm 42   1960 (Ms.)   dur. 2′   SAB   **W-294**
   Text: Dutch (Bible)
      Commission: Dutch Radio

Querela pacis   1979 (HARM)   dur. 12′   SATB div   **W-295**
   (Complaint of Peace)
   Text: Latin (Desiderius Erasmus)
        1. Ad bellum gestis (You Are Going to War);
        2. Sed audio (But I Hear); 3. Apello vos (I Call
        You)
      Dedication: Association for the Good European
         Choirs (25th anniversary)
      Premiere: 31 May 1980, The Hague, European
         Youth Choir, Anton de Beer, conductor

Requiem (Introitus)   1978 (CSP vol. 1 - HARM)   dur. 5′   **W-296**
   SATB
   Text: Latin
      Dedication: Dr. Ludwig Strecker (in remembrance)

Rey van Gozewijn   1937 (Ms.)   dur. 2′   SSATB   **W-297**
   (Chorus of Gozewijn)
   Text: Dutch (Joosten van den Vondel)

Rijck God, Wien sal ick claghen   1985 (CSP vol. 7 - HARM)   **W-298**
    dur. 2′30″   SATB
   (Kingdom of God, to Whom Shall I Cry?)
   Text: Dutch (anon.)

Satire   1987 (CSP vol. 7 - HARM)   dur. 1′   SATB   **W-299**
   Text: German (Heinrich Heine)

Three Serious Songs   1983 (CSP vol. 7 - HARM)   SATB   **W-300**
        1. Waldlied - dur. 4′ (text: German [Nikolaus Lenau]);
        2. Priere blanche - dur. 2′ (text: French [Maurice
        Maeterlinck]); 3. Anguish - dur. 2′30″ (text: English
        [Pär Lagerkvist])
      Premiere: May 1984, European Youth Music
         Festival, Neerpelt, Belgium

Tristis est anima mea   1987 (CSP vol. 7 - HARM)   dur 3′10″   **W-301**
   SATB
   Text: Latin

Vaste gezangen uit Nocturne 5   1957 (DO)   Unison   W-302
(Ordinary of the Mass)
Text: Dutch
      1. Kyrie; 2. Gloria; 3. Sanctus; 4. Benedictus;
      5. Agnus Dei

De vechter   1939 (DO)   dur. 3'   SATB   W-303
(The Fighter)
Text: Dutch (Adama van Scheltema)

Vier geestelijke liederen   1941 (BA)   SATB   W-304
(Four Sacred Songs)
Text: Dutch (anon.)
      1. Kerstlied (Christmas Song) dur. 3';
      2. Driekoningenlied (Epiphany) dur. 2'; 3. O ghi,
      die Jezus wijngaert plant (O Thee, Who Plants
      Jesus' (Vineyards) dur. 3'; 4. Goede Jezus wees
      ons bi (Good Jesus Be With Us) dur. 4'

Vier volksliederen   1947 (HARM)   dur. 10'   SATB   W-305
(Four Folksongs)
Text: Dutch (anon.)
      1. Pools volkslied "Brünstige Lohe" (Polish
      Folksong); 2. De meisjes van Duinkerken (The
      Girls of Duinkerken); 3. Het Kwezelke (The
      Sanctimonious Person); 4. Daar was een Wuf die
      Spon (There Was a Girl Spinning)

Vier volksliederen   1948 (Z)   dur. 7'   SATB   W-306
(Four Folksongs)
Text: Dutch
      1. Kerstlied (Christmas Song); 2. Daar was een
      sneeuwwit vogeltje (There Was a Snow-White
      Little Bird); 3. Pierlala (Puppet); 4. Sarie Marais

Vijfstemmige canon   1973 (Ms.)   Unison   W-307
(Five-Voice Canon for the New Year)

Vocalizzo Burlesco   1978 (CSP vol. 1 - HARM)   dur. 5'   W-308
  SATB div
Vocalise (Henk Badings)

Voici le bois   1978 (CSP vol. 1 - HARM)   dur. 1'30''   SATB   W-309
(Here Are the Woods)
Text: French (Pierre de Ronsard)

Wach auf, meins Herzens schöne   1978 (CSP vol. 1 - HARM)   **W-310**
  dur. 2′   SSATTBB
(Wake Up, My Love)
Text: German (anon.)

Weer is de tuin van Hugten   1972 (Ms.)   four-voice canon   **W-311**
(Once Again in the Garden of Hugten . . .)

Des winters als het regent   1950 (HARM)   dur. 2′   SATB   **W-312**
(In the Winter When It Is Raining)
Text: Dutch (anon.)

With All Good Wishes   1966 (Ms.)   canon for four equal voices   **W-313**

Zwei Chorlieder   1977 (Ms.)   dur. 6′   **W-314**
(Two Choral Pieces)
Text: German (Hans Magnus Enzensberger)
        1. Schläferung (Sleepiness) - SSATBB; 2. Locklied
        (Song of Enticement) - SATB
        Commission: Youth Choir of Aachen, Germany
        Dedication: Hans Magnus Ensensberger
        Premiere: 28 April 1991, Youth Choir of Aachen,
          Germany, Fritz Ter Wey, conductor

Female Choir with
Symphony Orchestra

Ave maris stella   1965 (DO)   dur. 12′   SSAA   instr. perc,   **W-315**
  cel, arp, str. 5
(Hail, Star of the Sea)
Text: Latin (anon.)
        Dedication: Ria Bergmeyer
        Premiere: 10 July 1966, Kralings Female Choir,
          Ria Bergmeyer, conductor

Female Choir Unaccompanied

Ach Sorg du musst zurücke stahn   1978 (CSP vol. 3 - HARM)   **W-316**
  dur. 2′30″   SSA
(O Sorrow, You Must Stay Back)
Text: German (anon.)

Agnus Dei   1982 (HARM)   dur. 1'30''   for three equal voices   **W-317**
(Lamb of God)
Text: Latin

Au clair de la lune   1978 (CSP vol. 3 - HARM)   dur. 2'   SSA   **W-318**
(In the Moonlight)
Text: French (popular French)

Ave Maria   1978 (CSP vol. 4 - HARM)   dur. 3'   SA   **W-319**
Text: Latin

Ballade of Cocaine Lil   1978 (CSP vol. 3 - HARM)   dur. 5'20''   **W-320**
   SA div
Text: English (19th-century Chicago-Detroit)

Ballade van de twee koningskinderen   1983 (HARM)   **W-321**
   dur. 3'30''   SSA
(Ballad of the Two Royal Children)
Text: Dutch (anon.)
>   *Dedication:* Z. M. K. "Mea Dulcea," Bergen op
>   Zoom, Wim Steenbak, conductor
>   *Premiere:* 2 July 1983, The Hague, International
>   Choir Festival, AGEC

Benedictus   1982 (Ms.)   dur. 4'   Eight equal voices   **W-322**
Text: Latin

Canamus amici   1957 (HARM)   dur. 3'   SSAA   **W-323**
(Friends Let Us Sing)
Text: Dutch (Henk Badings); Latin (M. A. Schwartz)
>   (See *Mixed Choir* - **W-267**)

Daar was een sneeuwwit vogeltje   1978 (CSP vol. 3 - HARM)   **W-324**
   dur. 1'20''   SSAA
(There Was a Little Snow-White Bird)
Text: Dutch (German trans. by Henk Badings)

Drie liederen van Minne   1983 (CSP vol. 5 - HARM)   SSA   **W-325**
(Three Love Songs)
Text: Dutch (anon.)
>   1. Somer tijt (Summertime) dur. 2'; 2. Van de
>   twie ghelieven (About Two Lovers) dur. 2'; 3. Van
>   der Minne (Of Love) dur. 2'
>   *Dedication:* Female Youth Choir "Cantate," Venlo,
>   Netherlands, Gerard Franck, conductor

Est ist ein Ros entsprungen   1978 (CSP vol. 4 - HARM)   W-326
    dur. 2'   SA or SSA
(A Rose Is Just Blooming)
Text: German (Rochus von Liliencron)

Feuillage du coeur   1978 (CSP vol. 3 - HARM)   dur. 2'20''   W-327
    SSAA
(Heart Foliage)
Text: French (Maurice Maeterlinck)

Gelukwenscanon   1977 (Ms.)   for equal voices   W-328
(Congratulatory Canon)

Het lied van Isabella   1986 (HARM)   dur. 3'   SSA   W-329
    (Song of Isabella)
    Text: Dutch (Henk Badings)
        Premiere: 14 December 1986, Female Choir
           "Zanglust," Pieter van Moergastal, conductor

I Am a Poor Wayfaring Stranger   1978 (CSP vol. 4 - HARM)   W-330
    dur. 3'30''   SA
Text: English (North American); Dutch (Henk Badings)

Jubelstadje   1985 (Ms.)   dur. 2'   SSA   W-331
(Town of Joy)
Text: Dutch (Anton van Duinkerken)
        Dedication: City of Bergen op Zoom (jubilee
        celebration)
        Premiere: 11 April 1987, Z. M. K. "Mea Dulcea,"
        Wim Steenbak, conductor

Kyrie eleison   1979 (CSP vol. 4 - HARM)   dur. 4'   SSA   W-332
    Text: Greek, from Mass Ordinary
        Dedication: European Youth Music Festival,
        Neerpelt, Belgium

Kyrie incantationes et meditationes   1981 (EFN)   dur. 4'   W-333
    for two voices
Text: Greek and Latin
        Dedication: Hellmut Schoell, European Youth
        Music Festival, Neerpelt, Belgium

Le Corbeau et le renard   1978 (CSP vol. 4 - HARM)   dur. 2'   W-334
    SA
(The Raven and the Fox)
Text: French (La Fontaine)

Maria ging zware van kinde   1983 (Ms.)   for four equal voices   **W-335**
(Mary Went Pregnant With Child)
Text: Dutch (anon.)

Mater cantans filio   1978 (CSP vol. 3 - HARM)   dur. 4'30'' SSA   **W-336**
(Mother Singing to Her Son)
Text: Latin (anon.)

Nachtgesang   1986 (HARM)   dur. 2'   SSA   **W-337**
(Nightsong)
Text: German (J. C. B. Eichendorf); Dutch (H. Badings)

Ode   1970 (Ms.)   for two voices   **W-338**
Text: Henk Badings
        Dedication: Alexander Voormolen (75th birthday)

Old English Love Song: Sweet Nymph   1983 (Ms.)   SSA   **W-339**

Pastorale   1985 (EFN)   dur. 2'30''   SA div   **W-340**
Text: German (Horst H. W. Müller)
        Dedication: European Youth Music Festival,
                Neerpelt, Belgium

Psaume 42   1978 (CSP vol. 4 - HARM)   dur. 3'30''   SSA   **W-341**
(Psalm 42)
Text: French and Dutch

Requiem (Tractus)   1978 (CSP vol. 3 - HARM)   dur. 2'34''   **W-342**
SSAA div
Text: Latin
        Dedication: Dr. Ludwig Strecker (in remembrance)

Sicut lilium   1978 (CSP vol. 3 - HARM)   dur. 2'30''   SSA   **W-343**
(Like a Lily)
Text: Latin (Hooglied II, 2)

The Song of Lovers   1978 (CSP vol. 3 - HARM)   dur. 1'30''   **W-344**
    SSAA
Text: English (Iraqi, 13th century)

Stabat Mater   1954 (DO)   dur. 10'   SSAA with soprano solo   **W-345**
(also boy choir)
Text: Latin (Jacopo da Todi)
        Premiere: 13 April 1954, Jacobuskerk, The Hague;
                also, 24 April 1954, Opening of the Music Hall
                in the Vatican, Rome, Italy by "Laudate Pueri,"
                Brother Diogène (Huub Luiten), conductor

Tria amoris carmina 1983 (CSP vol. 6 - HARM) SSA   **W-346**
(Three Songs of Love)
Text: Latin
    1. Ave formosissima (Goodbye, Most Beautiful
    One) dur. 2'; 2. Veni, veni, venias (Come, Come,
    May You Come) dur. 1'30''; 3. Si puer cum
    puellula (If a Boy with a Girl) dur. 1'
    Dedication: Female Youth Choir "Cantate," Venlo,
    Netherlands, Gerard Franck, conductor

Trois Ballades 1951 (DO) SSAA   **W-347**
(Three Ballads)
Text: French
    1. Les Cydalias - Guy de Nerval dur. 3'50''; 2. L'Archet
    (The Bow) - Ch. Cros dur. 5'23''; 3. L'Oiseau de
    la tour (The Bird of the Tower) - J. Tellier dur. 4'26''
    Award: Radio Paris, France, 1950
    Premiere: 9 January 1952, Paris

Trois Chansons d'amour 1983 (CSP vol. 6 - HARM) SSA   **W-348**
(Three Songs of Love)
Text: French
    1. L'Occasion manquée (The Missed Opportunity)
    dur. 3'; 2. J'ai descendu dans mon jardin (I Went
    Out in My Garden) dur. 1'; 3. Réveillez-vous, belle
    endormie (Awake, Beautiful Sleeper) dur. 2'
    Dedication: Female Youth Choir "Cantate," Venlo,
    Netherlands, Gerard Franck, conductor

Trois Chants populaires 1953 (DO) SSAA with soprano solo   **W-349**
(Three Popular Christmas Songs)
Text: French (anon.)
    1. Noël nouvelet dur. 2'30''; 2. A la venue de
    Noël (On the Arrival of Christmas) dur. 2'; 3. Les
    Anges dans nos campagnes (Angels We Have
    Heard on High) dur. '
    Dedication: Brother Diogène (Huub Luitjen)
    Premiere: Radio Paris

Vier geestelijke liederen 1936 (BP)   **W-350**
(Four Sacred Songs)
Text: Dutch (anon.), Greek

Vier geestelijke liederen - (*continued*)

> 1. Hi truer die truren wil! (Let Him Grieve Who Wants to Grieve) dur. 1'30'' SS; 2. Ic draech dat liden verborghen (I Carry That Sorrow Hidden) dur. 2' SSA; 3. Kyrie eleison dur. 5' SSAA; 4. Ons is gheboren een kindekijn (To Us Is Born a Little Child) dur. 5' SSAA
>
> *Dedication:* Mevr. Karin Kwant-Törngren

Zes oude kerstliederen 1950 (HARM) SSAA   W-351
(Six Old Christmas Songs)
Text: Dutch (anon.)

> 1. Stille Nacht (Silent Night) dur. 2'; 2. Gloria in excelsis Deo (Glory to God in the Highest) dur. 2'; 3. Nu sijt wellecome (Now Be Welcome) dur. 2'; 4. Een rose fris ontloken (A Rose Has Just Bloomed) dur. 2'; 5. Ghy syt uitverkoren (Ye Are Chosen) dur. 2'; 6. Maria ghing zware van kinde (Mary Went Pregnant With Child) dur. 1'

De zoom 1985 (Ms.) dur. 2'30'' SSA   W-352
Text: Dutch (Anton van Duinkerken)

> *Dedication:* Z. M. K. "Mea Dulcea," Bergen op Zoom, Wim Steenbak, conductor

Male Choir with Symphony Orchestra

St. Mark Passion 1971 (DO) dur. 55' TTBB solo, TTBB/   W-353
TTBB and narrator   instr. 2222-3330 - timp, perc 3, cel, str. 5, tape
Text: English (Bible)

> *Commission:* Dutch Government
> *Dedication:* Jos Vranken
> *Premiere:* 18 May 1972, Rotterdam

Te Deum 1962 (DO) dur. 25' TTBB instr. 3222-4431 -   W-354
timp, perc, cel, pf, str. 5
(We Praise You, O God)
Text: Latin (anon.)

> *Dedication:* C. Receveur

Male Choir with Wind Orchestra

Cantata 5   *Laus pacis*   1956 (DO)   dur. 30′   for soprano   **W-355**
  solo and male choir   instr. 212 + bass cl., 1 - 2331 -
  timp, perc, cel, (pf), cb
(Praise of Peace)
Text: Latin (Desiderius Erasmus)
      1. Introduzione; 2. Recitativo; 3. Aria; 4. Intermezzo;
      5. Recitativo; 6. Fuga; 7. Rondo; 8. Esclamazione;
      9. Finale
      Commission and Dedication: "Venlona"

Trompetstemming   1974 (DO)   dur. 8′   madrigal for male   **W-356**
  choir   instr. 2 + pic, 1,4 + E♭ cl. + bass cl., 1 - 3 sax
  (atb) - 32 + 3 cornets,3 + 2 bar., 2 - timp, perc 3, cb
(Trumpet Tuning)
Text: Dutch (Pierre Kemp)
      1. Allegro for Orchestra; 2. Allegro for Choir and
      Orchestra
      Commission: Dutch Radio
      Premiere: 22 October 1974, H. Dieteren, conductor

Male Choir with a Few Instruments

Genesis   1967 (DO)   dur. 22′   TB solo and TTBB choir   **W-357**
  instr. perc 4 and tape
(in the 31-tone system)
Text: English (Bible)
      Commission: Dutch Government
      Dedication: Haghe Sanghers, The Hague, Jos
        Vranken, conductor

Lucebert-Liederen   1963 (DO)   dur. 13′   for male choir and   **W-358**
  2 electronic sound tracks
Text: German/English (Lucebert)
      1. Das bisschen Wirklichkeit (A Little Reality);
      2. The Tobacco Frames the Lips; 3. Der Tau läutet
      die Blumen ein (The Dew upon the Flowers);
      Commission: Haghe Sanghers, The Hague
      Premiere: 24 May 1964, Haghe Sanghers, The
        Hague, Jos Vranken, conductor

Male Choir Unaccompanied

Ach Elslein, liebes Elselein   1978 (CSP vol. 2 - HARM)   W-359
 dur. 2'30''   TTB
(O Elslein, Dear Elselein)
Text: Dutch

Auprès de ma blonde   1966 (HARM)   dur. 5'   TTBB   W-360
(Near My Blonde One)
Text: French (anon.)

Ave Regina caelorum   1978 (CSP vol. 5 - HARM)   dur. 3'   W-361
 TTBB
(Hail, Queen of Heaven)
Text: Latin (anon.)
     Premiere: 15 November 1981, Bergen op Zoom,
        "Fortissimo," Wim Steenbak, conductor

La Bergère aux champs   1982 (CSP vol. 5 - HARM)   dur. 2'   W-362
(The Sheperdess in the Fields)
Text: French (anon.)
     Dedication and Premiere: 16 April 1983, "Fortissimo,"
        Bergen op Zoom, Wim Steenbak, conductor

The Blue-Tail Fly   1978 (CSP vol. 2 - HARM)   dur. 2'30''   W-363
 TTBB
Text: English (North America)

Canon voor gelijke stemmen   1976 (Ms.)   W-364
(Canon for Equal Voices)
     Dedication: Marius Monnikendam

Carmina stultitiae   1964 (KNZB)   TTBB   W-365
(Songs of Folly)
Text: Latin (Desiderio Erasmus)
     1. Inscriptio (Inscription) dur. 3'; 2. Stultitiae loquitur
     (Folly Speaks) dur. 2'30''; 3. Stultitiae viri (Folly
     of Man) dur. 2'30''
     Commission: Dutch Government

Chanson de Bourgogne en rondeau   1982 (CSP vol. 5 - HARM)   W-366
 dur. 3'30''   TTBB
(Song of Burgundy in Rondo)
Text: French (anon.)
     Dedication and Premiere: 16 April 1983, Bergen op
        Zoom, "Fortissimo," Wim Steenbak, conductor

Don Bosco cantate   1947 (Ms.)   dur. 8′   three-voice male choir   **W-367**
    Text: Dutch (Bernard Verhoeven)
        1. Allegro moderato; 2. Lento; 3. Allegro molto

Drei geistliche Lieder auf altniederlandischen Texten und   **W-368**
   Melodien   1950 (HARM)   TTBB
    (Three Sacred Songs to Old Dutch Texts and Melodies)
    Text: German (anon.)
        1. Karfreitag (Good Friday) dur. 2′30″; 2. Ostern
        (Easter) dur. 2′30″; 3. Gebet (Prayer) dur. 2′30″

De driekusman   1965 (HARM)   dur. 2′30″   five voice male   **W-369**
   choir
   (The Street Musician)
   Text: Dutch (anon. and Henk Badings)

Drie liederen op teksten van P. C. Boutens   1947 (DO)   TTBB   **W-370**
    (Three Songs to Texts to P. C. Boutens)
    Text: Dutch
        1. Hart en Land (Heart and Country) dur. 3′;
        2. Nocturne triste dur. 3′; 3. Mey-liet (May Song)
        dur. 3′30″

Drie mannenkoren op de teksten van de zuster van gansoirde   **W-371**
   1947 (BA)   TTBB
    (Three Male Choir Pieces to Texts of van Gansoirde)
    Text: Dutch (Zr. van Gansoirde)
        1. Ave Maria, Maghet reyn (Ave Maria, Virgin
        Pure) dur. 1′30″; 2. Och nu mach ic wel trueren
        (O Now I May Truly Grieve) dur. 1′; 3. Hi truer
        die trueren wil (He Who Wants to Grieve May
        Grieve) dur. 2′30″
        Dedication: Die Delftsche Sanghers

De eendracht van het land   1940 (Ms.)   dur. 2′   TTBB   **W-372**
    (The Unity of the Land)
    Text: Dutch (Jan Engelman)

Een klein weemoedig lied   1941 (DO)   dur. 3′   TTBB   **W-373**
   (A Little Sad Song)
   Text: Dutch (Jan Slauerhoff)
        Dedication: "Venlona"

Een meisje dat van Scheveningen kwam   1965 (KNZB)   **W-374**
   dur. 2′   TTBB

Een meisje dat van Scheveningen kwam - (*continued*)
(A Girl Who Came from Scheveningen)
Text: Dutch
 Dedication: Haghe Sanghers, The Hague

En 's avonds 1966 (HARM) dur. 1' TTBB   **W-375**
(In the Evening)
Text: Dutch (anon.)

Gebed (Almachtige Godt) 1978 (HARM) from *Valerius Tijd*   **W-376**
 dur. 4'30'' TTBB
(Almighty God)
Text: Dutch (Valerius)
 Dedication: Boxmeers Vocal Ensemble (25th
  anniversary), Theo Lamée, conductor

Gelukwens aan Jos Vranken sr. 1970 (Ms.) dur. 2' TTBB   **W-377**
(Congratulation to Jos Vranken Sr.)
Text: Dutch

Gij volckeren hoort aen! 1978 (HARM) from *Valerius Tijd*   **W-378**
 dur. 2' TTBB
(You People Listen!)
Text: Dutch (Valerius)
 Dedication: Boxmeers Vocal Ensemble (25th
  anniversary), Theo Lamée, conductor

Goeden avond 1966 (HARM) dur. 2' TTBB   **W-379**
(Good Evening)
Text: Dutch (trans. by H. van der Laan)

Gruselett 1978 (CSP vol. 2 - HARM) dur. 4' TTBB   **W-380**
Text: German (Chr. Morgenstern)

Het daghet uyt den oosten 1967 (KNZB) dur. 10' for   **W-381**
 eight voice male choir
(Day Breaks in the East)
Text: Dutch (anon.)
 Dedication: Jos Vranken Jr. and the male choir
  "Zwolle"

Het lied van Piet Hein 1963 (KNZB) dur. 3' five voice   **W-382**
 male choir
(Song of Piet Hein)
Text: Dutch (Jan Pieter Heye)
 Commission: Haghe Sanghers, The Hague

Hoe rij die boere 1966 (HARM)   dur. 2'30'' TTBB   **W-383**
(How the Farmers Ride)
Text: South African (anon.)

In memoriam 1947 (Ms.) dur. 2' TTBB   **W-384**
Text: Dutch (Christiaan Huygens)

In memoriam 1952 (DO) TTBB   **W-385**
Text: Dutch
    1. Mij, Heere, laat vrij gaan (Christiaan Huygens)
    dur. 1'30'' (Lord, Let Me Go); 2. Egidius, waer best
    u bleven? (anon.) dur. 4' (Egidius, Where Did
    You Go?); 3. 't En is van U hier nederwaard (Guido
    Gezelle) dur. 1'30'' (It Came upon Here from You)
    Dedication: Prof. Mekel (in remembrance)

Jagerslied 1933 (KNZB) dur. 4' TTBB   **W-386**
(Song of the Hunter)
Text: Dutch (P. C. Boutens)
    Dedication: Eduard Flipse

Jubilate Deo 1982 (CSP 5 - HARM) dur. 4' TTBB   **W-387**
(Praise to God)
Text: Latin (Psalm 66)
    Dedication: "Fortissimo," Bergen op Zoom, Wim
        Steenbak, conductor
    Premiere: 30 October 1982, Roosendaal, Netherlands,
        Choir Singers Festival of North Brabant and
        Zeeland "Fortissimo," Wim Steenbak, conductor

Kerelslied 1978 (CSP vol. 2 - HARM) dur. 4' TTBB   **W-388**
(Fighting Song)
Text: Dutch and German

Languentibus in purgatorio 1959 (DO) dur. 6'   **W-284a**
(Languishing in Purgatory)
Text: Latin (anon.)
three performance options (see *Mixed Choir* - **W-284**):
    1. mixed choir; 2. soloists SATTB; 3. TTB, soprano
    solo, alto solo
    Dedication: To the Holy Father Pope John XXIII

Liederenbundel 1940 (A) for 2 eight-voice male choirs   **W-389**
(Song Cycle)
Text: Dutch

Liederenbundel - (*continued*)
>   1. Drinklied (Drinking Song) (anon.) dur. 1';
>   2. Schertslied (Satirical Song) (anon.) dur. 1'30'';
>   3. Dorserslied (Threshing Song) (René de Clerq)
>   dur. 2'; 4. Rouwlied (Mourning Song) (anon.)
>   dur. 2'30''; 5. Ruiterlied (Horseman's Song)
>   (anon.) dur. 1'30''; 6. Drinklied (Drinking Song)
>   (anon.) dur. 1'30''; 7. Rouwlied (Het Aschkruis -
>   Cross of Ashes) dur. 3'; 8. Zeemanslied (Sailor's
>   Song) (Hoffman von Fallersleben) dur. 4'

Lied op het ontzet van Leiden   1979 (EFN)   dur. 2'   TTBB   W-390
or SATB
(Song of the Liberation of Leiden)
Text: Dutch (Valerius)
>   *Dedication:* European Youth Music Festival,
>   Neerpelt, Belgium

Liefdeslied   1984 (Ms.)   dur. 3'   TTBB   W-391
(Love Song)
Text: Dutch (from old English by Henk Badings)
>   *Dedication:* Horster Male Choir - jubilee celebration

Dat liet van den Rhijnscen wijn   1934 (LTC)   dur. 3'   TTBB   W-392
(Song of the Rhine Wine)
Text: Dutch (P. C. Boutens)

Loch Lomond   1966 (HARM)   dur. 2'30''   Bar. solo and TTBB   W-393
Text: English (anon.) — Scottish folksong

Marche des vagabonds   1966 (HARM)   dur. 2'   TTBB   W-394
(March of the Vagabonds)
Text: French (anon.)

Notturno   1978 (CSP vol. 2 - HARM)   dur. 4'30''   TTBB   W-395
Text: Italian (Michelangelo)

Ode aan Roeske   1946 (DO)   dur. 4'   TTBB/TTBB   W-396
(Ode to Roeske)
Text: Dutch (Henk Badings)
>   *Dedication:* Fred Roeske

Polnischer Winter   1982 (CSP vol. 5 - HARM)   dur. 4'   TTBB   W-397
(Polish Winter)
Text: German (H. W. Müller)

Dedication and Premiere: 16 April 1983, Bergen op
Zoom, "Fortissimo," Wim Steenbak, conductor

Psalm 27   1983 (HARM)   dur. 4'   TTBB   W-398
Text: English (Psalm 27, verses 1, 3, 4, 6)
  Commission: Wheaton College (Illinois) Mens Glee
  Club, Clayton Halvorsen, conductor (25th
  anniversary as conductor)
  Dedication: Prof. Clayton Halvorsen

Psaume Huguenot   1978 (CSP vol. 2 - HARM)   dur. 4'   TTBB   W-399
Text: Psalm 51 (De Marot, 1543)

Schimplied (Swijgt onbeschaemde al-berispers)   1978 (HARM)   W-400
  dur. 1'30''   TTBB
Text: Dutch (Valerius)
  Dedication: Boxmeers Vocal Ensemble (25th
  anniversary), Theo Lamée, conductor

Skolion van Seikilos   1982 (CSP vol. 5 - HARM)   dur. 2'30''   W-401
  TTBB
Text: Greek (Seikilos); Dutch (Badings)
In memoriam Anton Hartman
  Dedication and Premiere: 16 April 1983, Bergen op
  Zoom, "Fortissimo," Wim Steenbak, conductor

Slaet op den trommele   1978 (HARM) from *Valerius Tijd*   W-402
  dur. 3'   for four- to eight-voice male choir
(Beat the Drums)
Text: Dutch (A. D. Vos, 1566)
  Dedication: Boxmeers Vocal Ensemble (25th
  anniversary), Theo Lamée, conductor

Sonnet van Petrarca   1982 (CSP vol. 5 - HARM)   dur. 1'30''   W-403
Text: Italian (Petrarca)
  Dedication: "Fortissimo," Bergen op Zoom, Wim
  Steenbak, conductor

Ten Green Bottles   1966 (HARM)   dur. 2'30''   TTBB   W-404
Text: English (anon.)

Trois Chants populaires (Three Noëls)   1950 (DO)   W-405
Text: French (anon.)
  1. Minuit sonne au clocher blanc (Midnight Sounds
  in the White Belfry) dur. 1'30''; 2. O nuit, heureuse
  nuit (O Night, Happy Night) dur. 2'30''; 3. Gai
  Rossignol sauvage (Happy Wild Nightingale) dur. 3'
  Commission: Dutch Radio

Trois Romances   1950 (DO)   **W-406**
(Three Romances)
Text: French
    1. Voici les lieux charmants (Here Are the Charming
    Places; N. Boileau) dur. 3' TTBB; 2. Madrigal
    (Francis Carcs) dur. 1'30" TTB; 3. Lydia (Leconte de
    Lisle) dur. 2' TTB
    Commission: Radio Paris

Twee kerstliederen op 14de eeuwse teksten   1947 (BA)   **W-407**
(Two Christmas Songs to 14th-Century Texts)
Text: Dutch (anon.)
    1. Kerstleys (Christmas Antiphonal Song) dur. 2';
    2. Wildi horen singhen (Let the Trumpets Sound)
    dur. 3'30"

Twee visies op een gedicht   1985 (HARM)   dur. 3'   **W-408**
(Two Visions of a Poem)
Text: Dutch (Marc Zwijsen and E. Schoonhoven)
    1. Liefste moet het altijd zo zijn? (Dearest, Does
    It Always Have to Be Like That?); 2. Chère
    Enfant faut-il toujours? (Dear Child, Does It
    Always Have to Be Like That?)
    Dedication: Oudenbosch Male Choir

Up i dee   1966 (HARM)   dur. 4'30"   TTBB   **W-409**
Text: English (anon.)

De vrouwenboom   1984 (Ms.)   dur. 3'   TTBB   **W-410**
(The Women's Tree)
Text: Dutch (J. Derix)
    Dedication: Horster Male Choir

Vier geestelijke liederen   1954   dur. 8'   TTBB   **W-411**
(Four Sacred Dutch Songs)
Text: Dutch (anon.)
    1. Hoe groot o Heer - Smeekbede (Supplication)
    (HARM); 2. In Jesu name - Nieuwjaarslied (New
    Years Song) (HARM); 3. Schoon boven alle
    schoen - Paaslied (HARM); 4. Heden is de grootste
    dag - Paaslied (Ms.) (Easter Song - Resurrection)

Vier kerstliederen   1952 (DO)   TTBB   **W-412**
(Four Christmas Songs)
Text: Dutch

1. Kom, zing een lied (Noel nouvelet) from *Trois Chants populaires* 1953 (see *Female Choir*) (Come Sing a Song) dur. 2'30''; 2. In de witte winternacht (Minuit sonne au clocher blanc) from *Trois Chants populaires* for male choir, 1950 (In the White Winters Night) dur. 1'30''; 3. O nacht (O nuit, heureuse nuit) from *Trois Chants populaires* for male choir, 1950 (O Night) dur. 2'30''; 4. O wilde nachtegale (Gai Rossignol sauvage) from *Trois Chants populaires* for male choir, 1950 (O Wild Nightingale) dur. 3'

Vier wereldlijke liederen   1954 (HARM)   TTBB   **W-413**
(Four Secular Dutch Songs)
Text: Dutch (anon.)
      1. Merck toch hoe sterck (Perceive How Strong)
      dur. 2'40''; 2. Schertslied (Satirical Song) dur. 1';
      3. Ballade (Ballad) dur. 2'40''; 4. Skotse Trije
      (Scottish Girl) dur. 2'

Vier weverkens   1966 (HARM)   dur. 2'   TTBB   **W-414**
(Four Weavers)
Text: Dutch (anon.)

Was braucht man auf ein'm Bauerndorf   1966 (HARM)   dur. 3'   **W-415**
   TTBB
(What We Need in a Farming Village)
Text: German (anon.)

6   OTHER VOCAL WORKS

Voice(s) with Piano

Ariettes méchantes, five songs   1944 (DO)   dur. 7'   **W-416**
   (Naughty Ariettes)
   Text: French (anon.)

Ariettes méchantes - (*continued*)
>1. Pastorale pour Jeannette; 2. Ariette; 3. Air sur une blonde; 4. Soupirs; 5. Vaudeville

Burying Friends, hommage à Francis Poulenc   1963 (DO)   dur. 5'   **W-417**
Text: English (K. Slessor)
>*Commission:* Alice Esty
>*Premiere:* 13 January 1964, New York, Alice Esty

Chansonnettes, six songs   1941 (AB)   dur. 9'   **W-418**
Text: French (anon.)
>1. Pastorale; 2. Musette; 3. Chansonnette; 4. Rondeau (Parodie); 5. Badinerie; 6. Tambourin

Chansons orientales, four songs   1942 (DO)   dur. 6'   **W-419**
Text: French (Li-Tai-Po and others)
>1. L'Indifférente (The Indifferent One); 2. La Jeune Fille nue (The Naked Young Girl); 3. Dernière Promenade (The Last Walk); 4. Sur les bords du Jo-yeh (On the Banks of the Jo-yeh)
>*Premiere:* Albert Dana, Amsterdam

Coplas   1942 (BP)   dur. 4'   **W-420**
Text: Dutch (H. de Vries)
>*Dedication:* Felix de Nobel
>(See *Voice(s) with Symphony Orchestra* - **W-449**)

Danklied   1970 (Ms.)   dur. 30''   **W-421**
(Song of Thanks)
Text: Dutch (Henk Badings)

Drie baritonliederen   1936 (DO)   dur. 5'   **W-422**
(Three Songs for Baritone)
Text: Dutch (Jan Engelman)
>1. Annabel; 2. Avondlijk zwijen (Silence at Evening); 3. Kleine air (Little Air)
>*Premiere:* Laurens Bogtman

Drie duetten   1936 (DO)   dur. 7'   for soprano and contralto   **W-423**
(Three Duets)
Text: Dutch (Hoffman von Fallersleben)
>1. Ghele bloemkens (Yellow Flowers); 2. Stil ende vredsaem (Still and Peaceful); 3. Hoe schone staet die linde (How Beautiful Is the Lime Tree)
>(See *Voice(s) with String Orchestra* - **W-446**)

Drie Dullaert-liederen 1935 (BP)   dur. 5'   for tenor   **W-424**
(Songs on Texts of Dullaert)
Text: Dutch (Dullaert)
      1. Petrus weenende (Peter Wept); 2. Christus
      bespot (Christ Mocked); 3. Christus stervende
      (Christ Dying)
      Dedication: Aan Ina
      Premiere: Amsterdam, Peter Pears and Benjamin
        Britten

Drie kerstliederen 1939 (DO)   dur. 10'   for soprano   **W-425**
(Three Christmas Songs)
Text: Latin (anon.)
      1. Dies est letitie (It Is a Day of Joy); 2. Puer
      nobis nascitur (A Boy Is Born to Us); 3. Ad
      festum letitie (To the Joyous Feast)
      (See *Voice(s) with Symphony Orchestra* - **W-450**)

Drie Rilke-liederen 1932 (DO)   dur. 3'   **W-426**
(Three Songs on Texts of Rilke)
Text: German (Rainer Maria Rilke)
      1. Das arme Kind (The Poor Child); 2. Es ist lang
      (It Is Long); 3. Das Märchen von der Wolke (The
      Tale of the Cloud)
      Dedication: Bertha Seroen

Eight Cummings Songs 1965 (DO)   dur. 20'   **W-427**
Text: English (E. E. Cummings)
      1. Spring! may - everywhere's here; 2. It may not
      always be so; 3. All in green went my love riding;
      4. If I have made, my lady; 5. Maggie and Millie
      and Molly and May; 6. Now (more near ourselves
      than we); 7. Dim i nu tio e; 8. I love you much
      Dedication: Alice Esty
      Premiere: 19 May 1966, New York, Alice Esty,
        soloist; W. Wilson, piano

Fünf Reich-Lieder 1974 (DO)   dur. 12'   **W-428**
(Five Songs on Texts of Reich)
Text: German (E. Reich)
      1. Was aus dir tönt (The Sounds You Make);
      2. Herbst (Autumn); 3. Nacht (Night); 4. Eine
      Welt ist zerbrochen (A World That Is Broken);
      5. Frühlingsabend (Spring Evening)
      Dedication: Etta and Willi Reich
      Premiere: Helga Schulz and Gerhard Huber

Fünf Rilke-Lieder   1978 (DO)   dur. 7'   **W-429**
(Five Songs on Texts of Rilke)
Text: German (Rainer Maria Rilke)
    1. Ernste Stunde (Quiet Hour); 2. Herbst (Autumn);
    3. Initiale (Initial); 4. Mondnacht (Moon Night);
    5. Schlusztück (Final Piece)

Liederen van de dood   1946 (DO)   dur. 9'   **W-430**
(Three Songs of Death)
Text: Dutch (anonymous, Leopold, Werumeus Buning)
    1. Egidius waar bestu bleven (Egidius, Where Did
    You Go?); 2. O, als ik dood, zal zijn (O, When I
    Will Be Dead); 3. Triomf van de dood (Triumph
    of the Dead)
    Dedication: Harry van Oss
    Premiere: 1949, Roos Boelsma

Dat liet van Alianora   1929 (Ms.)   dur. 3'   **W-431**
(The Song of Alianora)
Text: Dutch (P. C. Boutens)

Meiregen (ten children's songs)   1946 (DO)   dur. 15'   **W-432**
(May Rain)
Text: Dutch (M. Vos)
    1. Kom uit, Katrijntje (Come Out, Katrijntje);
    2. Meiregen (May Rain); 3. Zoo'n dommerd (Such
    a Fool); 4. Regendag (Rainy Day); 5. Vogelpret
    (Bird's Fun); 6. De merel (Blackbird); 7. Daar liep
    een knaapjen inde zon (A Lad Who Walked in the
    Sun); 8. Herfstdraden (Spider's Web); 9. Ring -
    Rang; 10. De zevenstar (The Constellation)

Minnedeuntje   Love Song   1937 (BP)   dur. 1'30''   **W-433**
Text: Dutch (Joosten van den Vondel)
    Premiere: Joh. Diepenbrock

Morgenstern-Lieder   1961 (DO)   dur. 10'   **W-434**
(Five songs for vocal quartet)
Text: German (Morgenstern)
    1. Fisches Nachtgesang (Fish's Evening Song);
    2. Das Huhn (The Chicken); 3. Das Mondschaf
    (The Moon Sheep); 4. Lunovis; 5. Das grosse
    Lalula (The Big Lalula)
    Commission: City of Amsterdam
    Premiere: 2 December 1961, Amsterdam

Die Mühle im Schwarzwäldertal 1974 (Ms.) dur. 1'30''   **W-435**
(The Mill in the Schwarzwälder Valley)
Text: German (anon.)

Najaarsnacht 1976 (Ms.) dur. 4'   **W-436**
(Song of Autumn)
Text: Dutch (A. Roland Holst)
    Commission: Roland Holst Foundation

Ode aan Aphrodite 1982 (Ms.) dur. 1'   **W-437**
(Ode to Aphrodite)
Text: Dutch (Henk Badings)

Ons ghenaket die avondster 1924 (Ms.) dur. 2'   **W-438**
(The Evening Star Comes Near to Us)
Text: Dutch (anon.)

Sechs Lechler-Lieder 1966 (DO) dur. 12'   **W-439**
(Six Songs on Texts of Lechler)
Text: German (Ottmar Lechler)
    1. Und es fällt der Regen (And the Rain Is Falling);
    2. Der Frühling ist's (It's Spring); 3. Du Innigkeit
    im Dämmerwald (You, Serenity in the Woods at
    the Light of Dawn); 4. Qualvoll dieses leise Weinen
    (How Painful Is This Quiet Weeping); 5. Irgendwo
    will man ganz ruhig, sein (Somewhere, You Want
    to Be Completely Quiet); 6. Das Schreiten Gottes
    wird zum Sturm (God's Strides Will Become a Storm)
    Premiere: 18 March 1967, Helga Schulz and
       Gerhard Huber

Twee Breman-liederen 1940 (AB)   **W-440**
(Two Songs on Texts of Breman)
Text: Dutch (Breman)
    1. Lied voor bewogen tijden (Song for Moving
    Times); 2. Nederlands volkslied (Dutch Folksong)

Twee Vildrac-liederen 1935 (DO) dur. 4'   **W-441**
(Two Songs on Texts of Vildrac)
Text: French (Vildrac)
    1. Chant du désespéré (Song of the Hopeless One);
    2. Chanson d'hiver (Song of Winter)
    Premiere: Hans Gruijs

Two Whale Songs 1980 (Ms.) dur. 6'   **W-442**
  Text: German (Horst H. W. Müller)
          1. Der Mensch (Man); 2. Der Wal (The Whale)
          Dedication: "Whale's Art"

Vier liedjies van weemoed 1948 (Ms.) dur. 7'   **W-443**
  (Four Songs of Melancholy)
  Text: South African (P. N. van Lijk Louw)
          1. Seemeeu (Seagull); 2. Ek hoor (I Hear);
          3. Dennebosse (Evergreens); 4. Liedje (Little Song)
          Premiere: Cornelis Kalkman

Vier wiegeliedjes 1936 (BP) dur. 5'   **W-444**
  (Four Cradle Songs)
  Text: Dutch (Hans de Vries)
          1. Die oogjes die sijn een wonder (The Eyes Are a
          Wonder); 2. Wanneer ik je draag in mijn armen
          (When I Carried You in My Arms); 3. Hier is een
          wieg voor kindje (Here Is a Cradle for the Child);
          4. De sterretjes aan den hemel (The Little Stars
          in Heaven)
          Dedication: Floortje en Loe
          Premiere: Amsterdam, Felix de Nobel and Annie
              Woud
          (See *Voice(s) with String Orchestra* - **W-448**)

Yvonne's wiegeliedje 1947 (Ms.)   **W-445**
  (Yvonne's Cradle Songs)
  Text: Dutch (Henk Badings)
          Dedication: Hetty Badings

Voice(s) with String Orchestra

Drie duetten 1936 (DO) dur. 7' for soprano and contralto   **W-446**
      instr. st. 5
  (Three Duets)
  Text: Dutch (Hoffman von Fallersleben)
          1. Ghele bloemkens (Yellow Flowers); 2. Stil ende
          vredsaem (Quiet and Peaceful); 3. Hoe schone
          staet die linde (How Beautiful Is the Lime Tree)
          (See *Voice(s) with Piano* - **W-423**)

Gekwetst ben ik van binnen 1967 (Ms.) dur. 3' for baritone   **W-447**
    instr. str. 5
(My Feelings Are Badly Hurt)
Text: Dutch (anon.)
    Commission: Dutch Radio

Vier wiegeliedjes 1936 (DO) dur. 5' for soprano instr.   **W-448**
    str. 5 by F. de Nobel
(Four Cradle Songs)
Text: Dutch (Hans de Vries)
    1. Die oogjes die sijn een wonder (These Eyes Are
    a Wonder); 2. Wanneer ij je draag in mijn armen
    (When I Carried You in My Arms); 3. Hier is een
    wieg van't kindje (Here Is a Cradle for the Little
    Child); 4. De sterretjes van den hemel (The Little
    Stars in Heaven)
    (See *Voice(s) with Piano* - **W-444**)

Voice(s) with Symphony Orchestra

Coplas 1942 (DO) dur 5' for contralto instr. 2222-2200 -   **W-449**
    timp, str. 5
Text: Dutch (Hans de Vries)
    Dedication: Felix de Nobel
    (See *Voice(s) with Piano* - **W-420**)

Drie kerstliederen 1939 (DO) dur. 10' for soprano instr.   **W-450**
    2221-3220 - timp perc, cel, arp, str. 5
Text: Latin (anon.)
    1. Dies est letitie (It Is a Day of Joy); 2. Puer
    nobis nascitur (A Boy Is Born to Us); 3. Ad
    festum letitie (To the Joyous Feast)
    (See *Voice(s) with Piano* - **W-425**)

Liederen van dood en leven 1940 (DO) dur. 18' for tenor   **W-451**
    instr. 2232-3230 - timp, perc, cel, arp, str. 5
Text: Dutch (Boutens), French translation
    1. Bij een doode (Of a Dead Person); 2. Morgen
    (Morning); 3. Maanlicht (Moonlight); 4. Eindeloos
    (Endless)
    Dedication: Louis V. Tulder

's Morgens is den riep zo kold   1967 (Ms.)   dur. 1'   for   **W-452**
    soprano   instr. 1111-1000 - perc, str. 5
(Freezing Morning)
Text: Dutch (anon.)
    Commission: Dutch Radio

't Vloog een klein wild vogelken   1950 (Ms.)   dur. 2'   for   **W-453**
    contralto   instr. flute, str. 5
(The Small White Bird Flying)
Text: Dutch (anon.)
    Commission: Dutch Radio

Voice(s) and Other Instruments

Drie geestelijek liederen   1953 (DO)   dur. 18'   for contralto   **W-454**
    and organ
(Three Sacred Songs)
Text: Dutch (Jan Luyken); English (R. Mabry)
        1. Van Jesus de ware ruste (From Jesus, the True
        Peace); 2. Lied tot alle vermoeide zielen (Song for
        All Tired Souls); 3. Air

Drie Oud-Nederlandse liederen   1967 (DO)   dur. 8'   three   **W-455**
    songs for voice, flute and harp
Text: Dutch (anon.)
        1. Middeleeuws minnelied (Middle Ages Love
        Song); 2. Het daget in den Oosten (The Dawn
        Breaks in the East); 3. Het viel eene hemels douwe
        (Heavenly Dew Fell)
    Commission: Dutch Radio

Sextet 1 *Lentemaan   1931 (DO)   dur. 8'*   Three songs for
    alto, flute, cl, vl, vla, vlc
(Spring Moon)
Text: Dutch (P. C. Boutens)
        1. Als uit den Hartstocht van het avondrood (Out
        of the Passion of the Sunset); 2. Ik weet nu zet
        Uw schone deemoed in (Now I Know It, Start
        Your Sweet Humility); 3. Doove pijnen sidderseinen
        (Trembling Sweet Pains)
        (See **Sextet 1** - *Other Combinations* - **W-131**)

Sextet 3 1987 (DO) dur. 19′ for soprano, fl, cl, vl, cb, guit
    Verses from Tao Teh King by Lao Tsu
        1. The Embodiment of Tao; 2. Praise of Mystery;
        3. Life in Love; 4. The Genesis of Forms; 5. Warning
        against War
        Dedication: Douglas Hensley
        Premiere: September 1987, Ensemble Iskra, San
            Francisco
        (See **Sextet 3** - *Other Combinations* - **W-133**)

Three Sacred Songs 1950 (DO) dur. 14′ for contralto,   **W-456**
    oboe, and organ
  Text: English (anon.)
        1. When Christ Was Born; 2. I Sing of a Maiden;
        3. Adam Lay y'bounden
        Dedication and Premiere: Akke de Vries

Declamatorio

Als een goet instrument 1938 (Ms.) dur. 15′ instr. fl, ob,   **W-457**
    vl, vla, organ
  Text: Dutch (Vorster)
        1. Preludium for organ; 2. Narration with organ;
        3. Canzona for oboe and organ; 4. Narration for
        violin, viola, and organ; 5. Intermezzo for violin
        and organ; 6. Narration for flute, violin, viola,
        and organ; 7. Finale, fugue for flute, oboe, violin,
        viola, and organ
        Commission: Dutch Radio
        Dedication: Queen Wilhelmina (jubilee celebration)

Ballade van de watersnood 1953 (DO) dur. 5′ for narrator   **W-458**
    and piano
  (Ballad of the Flooding Water)
  Text: Dutch (Werumeus Buning)

Les Elfes 1948 (DO) dur. 8′ instr. 3222-3330 - perc, arp,   **W-459**
    cel, str. 5
  (The Elves)
  Text: French (Leconte de Lisle)

Les Elfes (*continued*)
> *Commission and Dedication:* Iris Zeilinga-
> Doodeheefer
> *Premiere:* 1949, Italy

Geluid van de werkelijkheid   1958 (Ms.)   duration of the   W-460
>   musical items - 45'; duration of the whole piece - 120'
> electronic music: 2 tracks
> (Sounds of Reality)
> Text: Dutch (Hans Andreus, Remco Campert, Lucebert,
>   Vinkenoog, and others
> > 1. Introduction; 2. Associates 1; 3. Funeralia;
> > 4. Sarabande; 5. Sarabande 2; 6. Ragtime 1;
> > 7. Ragtime 2; 8. Ragtime 3; 9. Ragtime (Slot);
> > 10. In Concrete; 11. Overgang; 12. Associates 2;
> > 13. Retrospective; 14. Intermezzo; 15. Aeolische
> > zang 1; 16. Aeolische zang 2; 17. Apotheose;
> > 18. Apotheose (Finish)
> > *Commission:* Academy of Arts, Amsterdam
> > *Premiere:* 2 March 1958, Amsterdam

Kerstdeclamatorium   1952 (Ms.)   dur. 40'   instr. fl, ob,   W-461
>   string quartet
> (Christmas Narration)
> Text: Dutch (A. Horsting-Boerma)
> > 1. Inleiding, Verkondiging, Intermezzo (Introduction);
> > 2. Joseph, Intermezzo; 3. Tocht naar Bethlehem,
> > Intermezzo (Pastorale) (Journey to Bethlehem); 4. De
> > Herders, Intermezzo (Gavotte) (The Shepherds);
> > 5. De Wijsen uit het Oosten en Herodes (The Wise
> > Men of the East and Herod)
> > *Commission:* Dutch Radio
> > *Premiere:* 1952, Hilversum

Polly Picklenose   1969   dur. 2'   for narrator and tape   W-462
> Text: English (L. F. Jackson)
> > *Commission:* Heinz Corporation, Pittsburgh, U.S.
> >   (centennial celebration)
> > *Dedication:* Robert Boudreau
> > *Premiere:* 14 June 1969, Pittsburgh

De westenwind   1936 (DO)   dur. 9'   instr. 2221-4221 - perc,   W-463
>   arp, cel, pf, str. 5
> (The Western Wind)
> Text: Dutch (Geerten Gossaert)

7 ORGAN WORKS

Solo

Apparizioni 1977 (Ms.) dur. 10′   **W-464**
    Dedication: Hans Georg Pfluger
    Premiere: 10 August 1977, Eindhoven, Netherlands,
        Hans Georg Pfluger, soloist

Introduction, Chorale and Finale 1975 (DO) dur. 3′   **W-465**
On "Morning Has Broken"
    Dedication: Fred Tulan

Passacaglia piccola 1979 (BA) dur. 8′   **W-466**
    Dedication: Hellmut Schoell

Prelude and Arioso 1983 (DO) dur. 10′   **W-467**
    Dedication: Heidi Scheck

Preludium 1938 (DO) dur. 4′   **W-468**

Preludium en Fuga 1 1952 (DO) dur. 8′
    Premiere: 1952, Haarlem, Anton de Beer, soloist
    (See *31-Tone Temperament - Organ -* **W-486**)

Preludium en Fuga 2 1952 (DO) dur. 5′   **W-469**
    Dedication: Flor Peeters

Preludium en Fuga 3 1953 (DO) dur. 7′   **W-470**
    Dedication: Flor Peeters

Preludium en Fuga 4 1954 (DO) dur. 7′
    Commission: A. Fokker
    Premiere: 1955, Haarlem, Anton de Beer, soloist
    (See *31-Tone Temperament - Organ -* **W-487**)

Preludium on B.A.C.H.   1985 (Ms.)   dur. 3'   W-471

Quattro pezzi   1980 (BA)   dur. 10'   W-472
(Four Small Pieces)
      1. Monologo; 2. Preambolo; 3. Dialogo; 4. Cantilene

Ricercare   1973 (DO)   dur. 10'   W-473
    Dedication: Fred Tulan
    Premiere: 5 December 1973, New York, Fred
       Tulan, soloist

Toccata   1929 (DO)   dur. 5'   W-474

Variations on a Mediaeval Dutch Theme   1969 (DO)   dur. 12'   W-475
    1. Introduction; 2. Theme, l'istesso tempo; 3. Vivace;
    4. Tranquillo; 5. Chorale Fugue

With Instruments

Canzona   1938 (DO)   dur. 5'   for oboe and organ   W-476
    Premiere: August 1938, J. Stotijn

Canzona   1967 (DO)   dur. 5'   for French horn and organ   W-477

Canzona   1971 (DO)   dur. 5'   for trumpet and organ   W-478

Dialogues   1967 (DO)   dur. 5'   for flute and organ   W-480

Intermezzo   1938 (DO)   dur. 5'   for violin and organ   W-481

It Is Dawning in the East   1967 (DO)   dur. 15'   for guitar   W-482
    and organ
    1. Introduction; 2. Theme Pavan; 3. Ballad;
    4. Sarabande; 5. Agitato; 6. Intermezzo; 7. Chorale
    Fugue
    Commission: Claire Coci
    Premiere: 10 October 1967, New York, Clarie Coci,
      organist

Passacaglia   1958 (DO)   dur. 12'   for organ and timpani   W-483
  Dedication: Claire Coci
  Premiere: 1959, New York, Claire Coci, organist

Quempas   1967 (DO)   dur. 5'   for violin and organ   W-484a
  Also a version for viola and organ 1967 (DO)   dur. 5'   W-484b
    Premiere: 10 December 1967, Ludwigsburg, West
    Germany, G. Eisele and K. Komma, soloists

With Voice.   See **6** OTHER VOCAL WORKS

For 31-Tone Temperament

Archifonica   1976 (DO)   dur. 12'   W-485
  1. Demonstration; 2. Air; 3. Improvisation
  Commission: BUMA Festival of St. Louis, U.S.

Preludium en Fuga 1   1952 (DO)   dur. 8'   W-486

Preludium en Fuga 4   1954 (DO)   dur. 5'   W-487
  Commission: Adriaan Fokker
  Premiere: 1955, Haarlem, Anton de Beer, soloist

Reihe kleiner Klangstücke   1957 (DO)   dur. 24'   W-488
  1. Preludio; 2. Arietta; 3. Scherzo; 4. Sarabande;
  5. Siciliano; 6. Perpetuum mobile; 7. Recitativo;
  8. Pastorale; 9. Passepied; 10. Elegie
  Commission and dedication: Adriaan Fokker

Suite 1954   (DO)   dur. 12'   W-489
  1. Preludio; 2. Arietta; 3. Recitativo; 4. Interludio;
  5. Menuetto; 6. Postludio
  Commission: Adriaan Fokker
  Premiere: December 1954, Haarlem, Anton de Beer,
    soloist

8   CARILLON WORKS

Solo

Etude for Alternating Hands   1987 (Ms.)   dur. 1'30''   **W-490**
(3 octaves)
> *Commission:* Carillon School in Amersfoort,
>   Netherlands

Etude with Arpeggios   1987 (Ms.)   dur. 2'30''   **W-491**
(4 octaves)

Pedal Etude   1987 (Ms.)   dur. 2'30''   **W-492**
(4 octaves)

Preludio e Arioso   1977 (DO)   dur. 9'   **W-493**
(4 octaves)
> *Commission:* City of Dordrecht, Netherlands
> *Dedication:* Jaap van den Ende
> *Premiere:* 1978

Sonata 1   1949 (DO)   dur. 10'   **W-494**
(4 octaves)
> 1. Toccata; 2. Aria; 3. Fuga
> *Commission:* City of Rotterdam
> *Premiere:* 1949, Ferdinand Timmerman

Sonata 2   1950 (DO)   dur. 10'   **W-495**
(4 octaves)
> 1. Moderato; 2. Menuet (molto tranquillo);
> 3. Tamborin (Allegro vivace)
> *Premiere:* 1951, Belgium, by Staf Nees

Suite 1   1943 (DO)   dur. 8'   **W-496**
(3 octaves)
> 1. Preludium; 2. Air; 3. Rondo

Suite 2   1951 (BE)   dur. 10′   **W-497**
  (4 octaves)
            1. Toccata octofonica; 2. Aria hexafonica; 3. Rondo
            giocoso
            Award: Jef Denijn Prize, Malines, Belgium, 1952
            Dedication: Staf Nees
            Premiere: Belgium, by Staf Nees

Suite 3   1953 (BE)   dur. 10′   **W-498**
  (3 octaves)
            1. Preludium; 2. Scherzo; 3. Air; 4. Passacaglia
            Award: Malines, Belgium, 1954
            Premiere: 1954, Belgium, by Staf Nees

Suite 4   1953 (DO)   dur. 10′   **W-499**
  (3 octaves)
            1. Boerenschots (contradans); 2. Wals; 3. Boerenplof;
            4. Rielen
            Commission: City of Rotterdam
            Premiere: 14 July 1953, Ferdinand Timmerman

Suite 5   1983 (DO)   dur. 14′   **W-500**
  (4 octaves)
            1. Gaillarde; 2. Old Women's Dance; 3. Hornpipe;
            4. Sarabande for the Court; 5. Final Jigg (Double)
            Commission and Dedication: Jim Lawson
            Premiere: 1985, New York

9   THEATER MUSIC

Opera

Asterion, radio opera   1957 (Ms.)   dur. 75′   instr. 2320-3221 -   **W-501**
  perc 2, arp, pf, str. 5, el music

Asterion - (*continued*)
  Leading parts: Princess (sop), Asterion (ten), Magician (bass),
    mixed choir
  Text: South African (P. N. van Wijk Louw)
    Commission: South African Radio
    Premiere: 11 April 1958, Johannesburg, South
        Africa

Liefde's listen en lagen   1945 (DO)   dur. 120′   comic chamber   W-502
  opera in 3 acts   instr. 3221-3100 - perc, str. 5
  (Loves Ruses and Snares)
  Vocal parts: Annette (sop), Margriet (alto), Herman (ten),
    Antonius (bar), Rodrigo (bass)
  Text: Dutch/German (Henk Badings with Tom Bouws)
    Premiere: 6 January 1948, Netherlands, William
        van Otterloo, conductor

Martin Korda D. P.   1960 (DO)   dur. 150′   dramatic choral   W-503
  opera in 3 acts   instr. 3222-4331 - timp, perc 3, cel, str. 5,
  el music
  Leading parts: Wanda (sop), Mila Korda (sop), Wanda's
    mother (mezzosop), Martin's mother (alto), Martin
    Korda (ten), Stefan (bar), Josef (bass)
  Text: Dutch (Badings, Jan van Eyck)
    Commission: Dutch Government
    Premiere: 15 June 1960, Holland Festival, Amsterdam,
        Nederlandse Opera, William van Otterloo,
        conductor

De nachwacht   1942 (UE)   dur. 150′   dramatic opera in 3   W-504
  acts   instr. 2222-4330 - timp, perc, cel, arp, str. 5
  Leading parts: Saskia (sop), Rembrandt (bar), Captain
    Banning Cocq (bass)
  Text: Dutch/German (T. Bouws)
    Commission: City of Hamburg, Germany
    Dedication: G. Hertog
    Premiere: 13 May 1950, Antwerp, Belgium,
        Koninklijke Vlaamse Opera, Johannes den
        Hertog, conductor

Orestes, radio opera   1954 (Ms.)   dur. 60′   instr. 4343-4431 -   W-505
  sax 2, timp, perc, cel, pf, arp, str. 5, el music
  Leading parts: Hermione (sop), Pallas Athene (mezzo sop),
    Chlytaemnestra (alto), Pythia (alto), Orestes (ten),
    Pylades (nar), Apollo (bar), choir

Text: Dutch/German/English (Badings, Starink)
　　　1. Prologue; 2. Pastorale; 3. Melodrama; 4. March;
　　　5. Lamento; 6. Fantasy; 7. Episodo; 8. Passacaglia;
　　　9. Intermezzo; 10. Notturno; 11. Oracolo;
　　　12. Ostinato; 13. Piege; 14. Epilogue
　　　Award: Prix Italia
　　　Commission: Dutch Radio
　　　Premiere: 24 September 1954, Florence, Italy

Salto mortale　1959 (Ms.)　dur. 55′　instr. el music　　　**W-506**
　　Television Chamber Opera in 12 Scenes
　　Vocal parts: Giulia (sop), Etta (alto), Angeli (ten),
　　　Solano (bass), Prosector (bass)
　　Text: Dutch (Badings, Belcampo)
　　　　Award: Salzburg Award (1959)
　　　　Commission: Dutch Television
　　　　Premiere: 19 June 1959, Eindhoven, Netherlands

Ballet

Balletto grottesco　1939 (UE)　dur. 10′　for two pianos
　　　　1. Intrada; 2. Marcia funèbre; 3. Ballo; 4. Intermezzo;
　　　　5. Rondo populare; 6. Rumba
　　　　Commission: City of Rotterdam
　　　　(See **Compositions for Piano** - *Four Hands/Two
　　　　　Pianos* - **W-32**)

Balletto notturno　1975 (DO)　dur. 12′　for two pianos
　　　　1. Giaoco delle campone lontane (molto moderato);
　　　　2. Giaoco degli arabeschi sinnuosi (lento)
　　　　(See **Compositions for Piano** - *Four Hands/Two
　　　　　Pianos* - **W-33**)

Balletto serioso　1955 (DO)　dur. 25′　instr. 2232-4331 -
　　timp, perc, cel, pf, str. 5
　　(L'apparechio minacciante)
　　　　1. Introduzione (Lento); 2. Tempo di valsa; 3. Tema
　　　　con variazone; 4. Tempo di valse; 5. Largo
　　　　(Sarabande); 6. Marcia; 7. Aria; 8. Coda
　　　　Commission: Johan Wagenaar Foundation

Balletto serioso - (*continued*)
    Premiere: 7 January 1957, Rotterdam, National
    Dutch Ballet
    (See **Compositions for Piano** - *Four Hands/Two*
    Pianos - **W-34** and *Other Symphonic*
    Compositions - **W-157**)

Evolutions 1958 (Ms.)   dur. 14′ el music: 1 or 2 tracks   **W-507**
    1. Overture; 2. Air; 3. Ragtime; 4. Intermezzo;
    5. Wals; 6. Finale
    Commission: City of Hannover, Germany
    Premiere: 24 April 1959, Vienna, Austria, by
       Yvonne Georgi

Genesis 1958 (Ms.)   dur. 15′ el music: 1, 2 or 4 tracks   **W-508**
    1. Introduction; 2. Principal Part; 3. Finale
    Dedication: Philips Corp.
    Premiere: 7 October 1958, World Exposition,
       Brussels, Belgium

Jungle 1959 (Ms.)   dur. 20′ el music: 1 or 2 tracks   **W-509**
    Commission: Dutch Government
    Premiere: 1959, Amsterdam, by Rudi van Dantzig

Kain 1956 (Ms.)   dur. 18′ el music: 2 tracks   **W-510**
    Commission: Philips Corporation
    Premiere: 1957, Hannover, Germany

Orpheus en Eurydice (Orpheus und Euridike) 1941 (SM)   **W-511**
    dur. 90′; instr. 3333-4431 - timp, perc, cel, arp, str. 5
  Vocal parts: bar solo, nar, mixed choir
  Text: Dutch/German (Werumeus Buning, L. Andersen)
    Act 1 - Ouverture, Tans der Dienerinnen, Ode,
    Duett, Finale; Act 2 - Introduktion, Passacaglia,
    Tod Eurydike; Act 3 - Introduktion und Tans des
    Hades Lied des Orpheus, Gang zur Ober Welt;
    Act 4 - Introduktion, Klage des Orpheus; Finale:
    Tanz der Mänaden, Tod des Orpheus Furientans
    und Epilog
    Dedication: Yvonne Georgi
    Premiere: 17 April 1941, Amsterdam, Yvonne
       Georgi Ballet

Variations électroniques 1957 (Ms.)   dur. 10′ 1 track   **W-512**

The Woman of Andros   1959 (Ms.)   dur. 47'   1, 2, or 4 tracks   **W-513**
    1. Inleiding (Introduction); 2. Onderbroken feest
maal (Interrupted Dinner Party); 3. Solo Glycerium;
4. Milieu Pamphilus; 5. Gastmaal (Guest Meal);
6. Pas de deux (Two-Step); 7. Ontmoeting Pamphilus
(Meeting of Pamphilus Glycerium); 8. Solo Chrysis;
9. Afscheid Chrysis (Farewell Chrysis); 10. Dood
van Chrysis (Death of Chrysis)
Commission: Dutch Government
Premiere: 14 April 1960, Hannover, Germany,
    Yvonne Georgi Ballet

Incidental Music

Bolke de Beer   1957 (Ms.)   dur. 12'; instr. cl, trmb, cel, perc,   **W-514**
    concrete music on tape
Vocal parts: alto, bass
Text: Dutch (A. D. Hildebrand)
    1. Overture; 2. Lied van Bolke; 3. Noodlostmuziek;
4. Bosmuziek; 5. Lied v. d. Haas; 6. Nocturne; 7. Lied
van Bolke; 8. Bouwscène en Wals; 9. Telescene;
10. Krekelorkest; 11. Siciliene; 12. Cortège
Commission: Telefunken

The Countess Cathleen   1952 (DO)   dur. 15'; instr. 1110-0000 -   **W-515**
    perc, arp, pf, cel, str. 3, vocal part
Text: English (Yeats)
    1. Overture; 2. Scènemuziek; 3. Troubadourslied;
4. Lied van Aleal; 5. Scènemuziek; 6. Intermezzo;
7. Lied van Aleal; 8. Lied van Schemus; 9. Intermezzo;
10. Slotmuziek; 11. Inleiding; 12. Intermezzo;
13. Scènemuziek; 14. Scènemuziek; 15. Scènemuziek
and Slot
Commission: Catholic Radio Foundation
Premiere: Hilversum, Henk Badings, conductor

Gijsbreght van Aemstel   1937 (DO)   dur. 85'; instr. 2222-4220 -   **W-516**
    timp, perc, str. 5
Vocal parts: alto solo, choir
Text: Dutch (Joosten van den Vondel)
    Premiere: 1937, Amsterdam

Ifigeneia in Taurië   1951 (DO)   dur. 30'; instr. 1220-000 -   **W-517**
   perc, arp
Vocal parts: female choir, nar
Text: Dutch (Euripides-Nijhoff)
      1. Inleiding; 2. Intermezzo; 3. Paridos; 4. 1st
      Kommos; 5. 1st Stasimon; 6. 2nd Kommos; 7. 2nd
      Stasimon; 8. Offerstoet Tempelmuziek; 9. Vervolg;
      10. 3rd Stasimon; 11. Epilogue
      Commission: Dutch Government
      Dedication: Johan de Meester
      Premiere: 16 June 1951, Holland Festival

Lanceloet   1950 (DO)   dur. 15'; instr. 1110-1000 - str. 4   **W-518**
   Text: Dutch (anon.)
      Overture - 7 Intermezzi - Epilogue
      Commission: Catholic Radio Foundation
      Premiere: 14 November 1951

De nacht voor morgen   1956 (Ms.)   dur. 8'   el music: 3 tracks   **W-519**
   (The Night before the Morning)
   Text: Dutch (Gerrit Kouwenaar)
      Commission: Telefunken
      Premiere: 1 April 1956

De spreekcel   1959 (Ms.)   dur. 42'   el music: 1 track   **W-520**
   (The Telephone Box)
   Text: Dutch (van Eyck)
      Premiere: Sorrento, Italy

Turned On   1971 (Ms.)   theater piece for children   instr.   **W-521**
   2221-2220 - perc, tape
      Commission: Robert Boudreau
      Premiere: 1971

Film Music

Les achalunés   1960   **W-522**

The Flying Dutchman   1957   dur. 40'   el music: 1 track   **W-523**
      Commission: Dutch Government
      Premiere: 22 June 1957, Holland Festival

Hoelloch   1966   **W-524**

Indifference   1968   **W-525**

Secret Passion   1964   **W-526**

Sigmund Freud   dur. 5′   el music: 1 track   **W-527**

Sound and Image   1965   dur. 12′   **W-528**
      Award: Prize of the Australian Film Festival (1965)

Tronfølgern in Latin Amerika   1966   **W-529**

Variations électroniques   1957   dur. 10′
      Commission: Philips Corporation
      (See *Ballet* - **W-512**)

10 ELECTRONIC MUSIC

Armageddon   1968 (P)
      (See *Wind Orchestra* - **W-201**)

Capriccio   1959 (DO)   for solo violin and 2 tracks
      (See *Chamber Music* - **W-88**)

Chaconne   1965 (DO)   for B-flat trumpet and 1 track
      (See *Chamber Music* - **W-97**)

Concertino   1967 (DO)   for piano and 2 tracks
      (See *Compositions for Piano* - **W-38**)

Dialogues for Man and Machine   1958 (Ms.)   dur. 21′   **W-530**
  Text: English (Badings, Schaffy)
      1. Overture; 2. Air; 3. Ragtime; 4. Intermezzo;
      5. Scherzo; 6. Wals; 7. Finale
      Premiere: 1958, World Expo, Brussels, Belgium

Drei Schwärmereien   1964 (DO)
>   (See *Choral Works - Mixed Choir with a Few*
>   *Instruments* - **W-256**)

Electro-magnetic Sound Figures   1959   dur. 5'   1, 2, or 4 tracks   **W-531**
>   *Premiere:* 1959, Festival, Gravesano, Switzerland

Evolutions   1958 (Ms.)
>   (See *Ballet* - **W-507**)

The Flying Dutchman   1957   dur. 40'   1 track
>   (See *Film Music* - **W-523**)

Geluid van de werkelijkheid   1958 (Ms.)
>   (See *Declamatorio* - **W-460**)

Genesis   1958 (Ms.)
>   (See *Ballet* - **W-508**)

De hoorschelp   1958 (Ms.)   dur. 18'   **W-532**
> Text: Dutch (Jan van Eyck)

Jungle   1959 (Ms.)
>   (See *Ballet* - **W-509**)

Kain   1956 (Ms.)
>   (See *Ballet* - **W-510**)

Kontrapunkte   1970 (Ms.)   for piano and tape
>   (See *Compositions for Piano* - **W-39**)

Lucebert-liederen   1963 (DO)
>   (See *Male Choir with a Few Instruments* - **W-358**)

Martin Korda D. P. Act 3   1960 (DO)
>   (See *Opera* - **W-503**)

De nacht voor morgen   1956 (Ms.)
> (The Night before the Morning)
>   (See *Incidental Music* - **W-519**)

Op het tweede gehoor   1957 (Ms.)   dur. 12'   **W-533**
> (Upon the Second Hearing)
> Text: Dutch (Jan van Eyck)
>>   *Commission:* Opening of the Arts Academy,
>>   Amsterdam
>>   *Premiere:* 21 March 1957

Orestes (fragment) 1954 (Ms.)
       (See *Opera* - **W-505**)

Pittsburgh Concerto 1965 (P)
       (See *Wind Orchestra* - **W-215**)

Salto mortale 1959 (Ms.)
       (See *Opera* - **W-506**)

Sigmund Freud 1962 (Ms.)
       (See *Film Music* - **W-527**)

Sonatina 1955 (Ms.) dur. 4′   **W-534**
       1. Preludium; 2. Air; 3. Postludium
       Commission: Dutch Radio

Toccata 1 1964 (Ms.) dur. 3′ for 2 tracks   **W-535**

Toccata 2 1964 (Ms.) dur. 4′ for 4 tracks   **W-536**

The Woman of Andros 1959 (Ms.)
       (See *Ballet* - **W-513**)

11 ARRANGEMENTS OF FOLKSONGS

All arrangements were written 1949-50 and are in manuscript   instr. 1121-0110 -
    perc, arp, pf, str. 5
    Commission: Catholic Radio Organization

A moda gellega for choir   **W-537**
   Poem: Spanish (Helene Nolthenius)
   Dorpsdans (Village Dance)

Ach nichts ist weit und breit   for sorpano   W-538
   Poem: Bohemian (H. Pijfers)
   Niets is er wijd noch zijd (Nothing Is Wide and Broad)

Addio la caserma   for baritone   W-539
   Poem: Italian (Helene Nolthenius)
   Kazerne vaarwel (Farewell to the Military Base)

Adios, ene maitia   for tenor   W-540
   Poem: Spanish (Helene Nolthenius)
   Vaarwel, mijn lief (Farewell My Dear)

Ainhara   for baritone   W-541
   Poem: Spanish (Helene Nolthenius)
   De zwaluw (The Swallow)

Argizagi ederra   for baritone   W-542
   Poem: Spanish (Helene Nolthenius)
   Maanlicht (Moonlight)

Auf der Wiese   for choir   W-543
   Poem: Hungarian (H. Pijfers)
   Op de weide (In the Meadow)

Aus dem Ungarland   for baritone   W-544
   Poem: Hungarian (M. v. d. Plas)
   Uit het schone Hongarije (From Beautiful Hungary)

L'Avvelenato   for soprano or tenor   W-545
   Poem: Italian (Helene Nolthenius)
   De Gifmengster (The Poisoner)

Canso de Nadal   for soprano   W-546
   Poem: Spanish (H. Pijfers)
   Kerstlied (Christmas Carol)

Canso de sega   (1) for choir   W-547
   Poem: Spanish (Helene Nolthenius)
   Oogstlied (Harvest Song)

Canso de sega   (2) for baritone   W-548
   Poem: Spanish (Helene Nolthenius)
   Oogstlied (Harvest Song)

Canzone di zampagnari   for mixed choir   W-549
  Poem: Italian (H. Pijfers)
  Kerstlied uit Napels (Christmas Carol from Naples)

Chorinus kaiolan   for soprano   W-550
  Poem: Spanish (Helene Nolthenius)
  Vogeltje in de kooi (Little Bird in the Cage)

Coucou, canari jaloux   for tenor   W-551
  Poem: Swiss (Helene Nolthenius)
  Rataplan, dat komt er zo van (The Cuckoo, the Jealous Canary)

Cucu   for baritone and mixed choir   W-552
  Poem: Italian (Helene Nolthenius)
  Koekoek (Cuckoo)

Dormi, dormi bel bambin   for soprano   W-553
  Poem: Italian (Helene Nolthenius)
  Ga nu slapen kindje schoon (Go to Sleep Little Child)

Eine schöne gibt es nur   for baritone   W-554
  Poem: Hungarian (H. Pijfers)
  Slechts één liefste (Only a Dear One)

El pano moruno   for baritone   W-555
  Poem: Spanish (Helene Nolthenius)
  Het zwarte moorse laken (The Black Moorish Sheet)

En passant par la Lorraine   for soprano   W-556
  Poem: French (Helene Nolthenius)
  Met mijn klompen aan (With My Wooden Shoes)

La filadora   for soprano   W-557
  Poem: Spanish (Helene Nolthenius)
  Het Spinstertje (The Spinner)

Flog eine Falke   for tenor   W-558
  Poem: Macedonian (M. v. d. Plas)
  Eens vloog er en valk omhoog (A Falcon Flew Up)

Gentil coqu'licot   for soprano   W-559
  Poem: French (Helene Nolthenius)
  Eens moest ik in mijn tuintje zijn (Once I Had to Be in
    My Garden)

Hei, hier ein Hain   for high voice   W-560
    Poem: Slovenian (H. Pijfers)
    Hé, hier een weg (Here Is a Path)

I tre re   for baritone   W-561
    Poem: Italian (Helene Nolthenius)
    Drie Koningen (Three Kings - Epiphany)

Ich hab mei Muetli fast alles verloren   for tenor   W-562
    Poem: Swiss (Helene Nolthenius)
    Minnepijn (Love's Sweet Pain)

Im Oberland   for mixed choir   W-563
    Poem: Slavic (Helene Nolthenius)
    Boven in de bergen (High in the Mountains)

's Isch Aeben a Mönch uf Aerde   for tenor   W-564
    Poem: Swiss (Helene Nolthenius)
    Daar is er maar een op aarde (There Is Only One on Earth)

Izar ederra   for tenor   W-565
    Poem: Spanish (Helene Nolthenius)
    Dwaallicht (Will-o-the-Wisp)

La Jardinière du roi   for tenor   W-566
    Poem: Swiss (Helene Nolthenius)
    De hovenierster (The Lady Gardener)

De Jasmin   for tenor   W-567
    Poem: Greek (H. Pijfers)
    De jasmijn (The Jasmin)

Jean de Nivelle   for baritone   W-568
    Poem: French (Helene Nolthenius)
    Jantje van Leiden

Juche! (Will immer fröhlich sein!)   for tenor   W-569
    Poem: Slavic (Helene Nolthenius)
    Joeché

Kehr ich Abends heim   for tenor   W-570
    Poem: Slavic (Helene Nolthenius)
    Kom ik 's avonds thuis (When I Come Home in the Evening)

Keiner auch nicht einer for soprano   **W-571**
    Poem: Slovenian (H. Pijfers)
    Nergens op de hele wereld (Nowhere in the Whole World)

Des König's Abschied for bass   **W-572**
    Poem: Hungarian (H. Pijfers)
    Het afscheid van de Koning (The Farewell of the King)

Lied des Galeersträflings for baritone   **W-573**
    Poem: Hungarian (H. Pijfers)
    Lied van de Galeislaaf (Song of the Galley Slave)

Los wie d'Vögel liebli singe for soprano   **W-574**
    Poem: Swiss (Helene Nolthenius)
    Voorjaarsliedje (Spring Song)

Das Mädchen vom Amselfeld for baritone   **W-575**
    Poem: Slavic (Helene Nolthenius)
    Het meisje van het spreeuwenveld (The Girl from the
        Sparrow Field)

Malborough s'en va (French) for soprano or baritone   **W-576**
    Poem: French (Helene Nolthenius)
    Het lied van Malbroek (The Song of Malbrook)

Maria wandelte for soprano and mixed choir   **W-577**
    Poem: Slavic (Helene Nolthenius)
    Maria die wilde naar Engeland (Maria Wants to Go to
        England)

Marion et le dragon for baritone   **W-578**
    Poem: French-Swiss (Helene Nolthenius)
    Marie en de soldaten (Mary and the Soldiers)

Meine Geige for baritone   **W-579**
    Poem: Slavic (Helene Nolthenius)
    Mijn Balalaika (My Balalaika)

Monsieur vous êtes jeun homme for baritone   **W-580**
    Poem: French (Helene Nolthenius)
    De Huwelijksmakelaar (The Matchmaker)

Mutter   for soprano   W-581
  Poem: Slavic (Helene Nolthenius)
  Moeder (Mother)

Nana   for alto   W-582
  Poem: Spanish (Helene Nolthenius)
  Wiegenlied (Lullaby)

Nie war hoch am Himmel   for tenor   W-583
  Poem: Hungarian (H. Pijfers)
  Er was geen dag (There Was No Day)

Nun Adé   for baritone   W-584
  Poem: Slavic (Helene Nolthenius)
  Nu Vaarwel (Now Farewell)

La ploma de Perdiu   for baritone   W-585
  Poem: Spanish (Helene Nolthenius)
  De Kat en de Muis (The Cat and the Mouse)

Presents al nino Jesus   for tenor   W-586
  Poem: Spanish (H. Pijfers)
  Gaven voor het Kerstkind (Presents for the Christ Child)

Quattro cavai che trottano   for tenor   W-587
  Poem: Italian (Helene Nolthenius)
  Mijn gondel deint op en neer (My Gondola Rocks Back
    and Forth)

Rackoczi-Lied   for choir   W-588
  Poem: Hungarian (H. Pijfers)
  Ruiterlied (Horseman's Song)

Ritornello di lavendaja wasurouwenhive   for soprano   W-589
  Poem: Italian (Helene Nolthenius)
  Was vrouwenlied (Washers Song)

Sag, wie kann   for baritone   W-590
  Poem: Slavic (Helene Nolthenius)
  Ach hoe leef je (How Do You Live?)

Sag, wohin du Reiter   for tenor and choir   W-591
  Poem: Hungarian (H. Pijfers)
  Waarheen ruiter (Where Are You Going, Horseman?)

Sass einmal ein Häslein an dem Rain   for baritone   W-592
  Poem: Polish (H. Pijfers)
  't Haasje (The Rabbit)

Der Schlitter eilt for tenor   W-593
    Poem: Hungarian (H. Pijfers)
    De slede rijdt (The Sled Rides)

Schon drei Jahre liege ich krank for baritone   W-594
    Poem: Macedonian (M. v. d. Plas)
    Katja (I Have Been Ill for Three Years)

Schwarze Äuglein for tenor   W-595
    Poem: Slavic (Helene Nolthenius)
    Zwarte ogen (Black Eyes)

Seh ich dich mein Herzensliebchen for low voice   W-596
    Poem: Bohemian (H. Pijfers)
    Zie ik jou mijn allerliefste (Do I See My Dearest?)

Son tre mesi, che il Soldato for tenor   W-597
    Poem: Italian (Helene Nolthenius)
    Het lied van de Schildwacht (The Song of the Guard)

Spiel nur, o spiel for baritone   W-598
    Poem: Hungarian (H. Pijfers)
    Speel dan, o speel (Play Then, O Play)

Tarantella de la Bellona for tenor   W-599
    Poem: Italian (Helene Nolthenius)
    Romeinse tarantella (Roman Tarantella)

Trauer um die Jugend for soprano   W-600
    Poem: Macedonia (M. v. d. Plas)
    Als je wist, mijn liefste (If You Only Knew, My Dearest)

Die traurige Braut for alto or baritone   W-601
    Poem: Slavic (Helene Nolthenius)
    De treurige bruid (The Sad Bride)

Unterm Fenster for tenor   W-602
    Poem: Slavic (Helene Nolthenius)
    Onder het venster (Under the Window)

Der Untreue for alto   W-603
    Poem: Slavic (Helene Nolthenius)
    De Ontrouwe (The Unfaithful)

La va in Filanda for tenor   W-604
    Poem: Italian (Helene Nolthenius)
    Soldaten afscheid (Soldier's Farewell)

Der Wanderer   for mezzo-soprano or baritone   W-605
  Poem: Greek (H. Pijfers)
  De Zwerver (The Wanderer)

War ein schöner Bursche   for choir   W-606
  Poem: Hungarian (H. Pijfers)
  't Was een jonge kerel (It Was a Young Man)

Warum, Lena so stolz   for tenor   W-607
  Poem: Macedonian (M. v. d. Plas)
  (Waarom verbeeld je je (Why Do You Think So Highly
    of Yourself?)

Wasch in weisser Milch   for choir   W-608
  Poem: Slavic (Helene Nolthenius)
  (Wash in White Milk)

Wasserlein, kalt wie Eis   for middle voice   W-609
  Poem: Czech (Louis de Bourbon)
  Watertje (Little Lake)

Wiegenlied   for alto   W-610
  Poem: Slavic (Helene Nolthenius)
  Wiegenlied (Cradle Song)

Zigeunerlieder   1951 (Ms.)   dur. 12'30''   (arrangements of   W-611
    Dvořák songs for soprano and orchestra); instr.
    2222-3200 - timp, perc, arp, str. 5
        1. Má pisen zas mi láskousmi (Mon Chant d'amour
        résonne) (My Love Song Resounds); 2. Kterak
        trojhranec můj přerozkosne (Ah, combien mon
        triangle joyeusement sonne) (Oh, How My Triangle
        Joyously Sings); 3. A lesje tichy kolem kol (Autour
        de moi tout dort en paix) (Around Me All Sleeps
        in Peace); 4. Když mne staramatka (Quand ma
        mère m'apprenait (When My Mother Taught Me);
        5. Strune nala dena, hochutoc sevkole (Compagnon,
        viens vite, la ronde commence!) (Come Quickly,
        the Round Begins!); 6. Siroké rukavy a široké gate
        (Vetu simplement le tzigane) (Simply Clothed the
        Gypsy); 7 Dějte klec jestřábu (Au haut du mont
        Tatra) (On Top of Mount Tatra)

DISCOGRAPHY

S = Stereodisc   M = Monaural disc   CD = Compact disc

Armaggedon   (1968)   for soprano solo and wind symphony   **D-1**
    orchestra, with tape
    "New Brass Symphony"
    KP 101s (1970) Point Park College Rec.; Bayer BR
       100024 CD
           Carole Farley, soprano; American Wind Symphony
             Orchestra, Robert Boudreau, conductor

Ballade   (1950)   for flute and harp   **D-2**
    CD-320/BIS (6 and 8 November 1985)
           Robert Aitken, flute; Erica Goodman, harp; with
             works by Fran Doppler, François Joseph
             Naderman, and Marjan Mozetich

Ballade   (1950)   for flute and harp   **D-3**
    EMI 5C053-25128 S
           Abbie de Quant, flute; Edward Witsenburg, harp

Ballade   (1950)   for flute and harp   **D-4**
    "Masters of Flute and Harp," vol. 2
    Klavier KS 560
           Louise Di Tullio, flute; Susan McDonald, harp; with
             works by Joseph Lauber and Vincent Persichetti

Ballade (1950)   for flute and harp   **D-5**
  Phillips N00695R M; Radio Nederland 6808.050 M; Radio
    Nederland 6808.784 M
      Hubert Barwahser, flute; Phia Berghout, harp

Balletto grottesco (1936)   **D-6**
  Marhel MA 25027 S
    Hellmut Schoell, piano

Balletto notturno (1976)   **D-7**
  Marhel MA 25027 S
    Hellmut Schoell, piano

Canamus amici (1957)   **D-8**
  HMG HG 2833 S
      Consortium Vocale Twente, Jan Heymink Liesert,
        conductor

Canzona (1967)   **D-9**
  "Twentieth Century Works for Horn & Organ"
  S671/Crystal
      Ralph Lockwood, horn; Melanie Ninneman, organ; with
        works by Oreste Ravanello, Gardner Read, Heidi
        Scheck, Thomas Woehrmann, and Gunther Marks

Capriccio (1959)   for violin and tape   **D-10**
  "Evolutions & Contrasts"
  Limelight LS 85055 (1968); Phillips 835.056
    Joke Vermeulen, violin

Cavatina (1952)   for alto flute and harp   **D-11**
  Coronet S-1713
    Pellerite, flute; Webb, harp

Cavatina (1952)   for alto flute and harp   **D-12**
  "Masters of Flute and Harp," vol. 2
  Klavier KS 560
      Louise Di Tullio, flute; Susann McDonald, harp; with
        works by Joseh Lauber and Vincent Persichetti

Cavatina (1952)   for alto flute and harp   **D-13**
  Toshiba-EMI/LRS-657
      Peter Bondesen, flute; Hideko Bondesen, harp; with
        works by Louis Spohr, Life Thybo, Adrian
        Grigorevich Shaposhnikov, and Mikhail Ivanovich
        Glinka

Chansons orientales (1943)   **D-14**
"Anthologie van het Nederlandse Lied in de 20e Eeuw"
LSP 14514/CBS
  Hein Meens, tenor; Tilly Keessen, piano

La Complainte des âmes (1946) from *Trois Chansons* **D-15**
 bretonnes
Private recording 6810.945 S
  Gelre's Kamerkoor, Willem Verway, conductor

Concerto for Flute 1 (1956) for flute and orchestra **D-16**
 Philips A00789R M
  Henk van Oordt, flute, and the Leids Studentenorkest
  "Sempre Crescendo," conducted by the soloist

Concerto for Flute 2 (1963) for flute and wind band **D-17**
 RCA SR4s-3264 S; Coronet Rec. Co. 1724 S
  Levina Boehl, flute; American Wind Symphony
  Orchestra, Robert Boudreau, conductor

Concerto for Flute 2 (1963) for flute and wind band **D-18**
 Mirasound 499025 CD
  Raymond Delnoye; Flute Brabant Conservatorium
  Harmonieorkest, Jan Cober, conductor

Concerto for Flute 2 (1963) for flute and wind band **D-19**
 E-1398–E-1399/St. Olaf Records (recorded 7 September
 1985, 9 February 1986, 23 May 1986)
  Melanie Sever, flute; St. Olaf Band, Miles Johnson,
  conductor; with works by Arthur Pryor, Malcolm
  Arnold, Richard Wagner, Silvestre Revueltas,
  Claude Smith, Paul Tschesnokoff, Vincent
  Persichetti, Peter Tchaikovsky

Concerto for Harp (1967) for harp and orchestra **D-20**
"Netherlands Music"
CV CD 9 A6 CD
  Vera Badings, harp; Concertgebouworkest, David
  Zinman, conductor

Concerto for Harp (1967) for harp and orchestra **D-21**
 Donemus DAVS 6902 (1969)
  Phia Berghout, harp; Radio Filharmonisch Orkest,
  Willem van Otterloo, conductor

Concerto for Piano 1 (1939)   for piano and orchestra   **D-22**
    Donemus DAVS 7172/2 S
            Cor de Groot, piano; Radio Filharmonisch Orkest,
            Jean Fournet, conductor

Double-Concerto 1 for Two Violins (1954)   for two violins   **D-23**
    and orchestra
    Philips A00487L M
            Herman Krebbers and Theo Olof, violins; Residentie
            Orkest, The Hague

Concertino (1967)   for piano and two soundtracks   **D-24**
    Marhel MA 25022 S
            Hellmut Schoell, piano

Dialogues (1967)   for flute and organ   **D-25**
    Bis CD-160 CD
            Gunilla von Bähr, flute; Hans Fagius, organ

Epiphany (1979)   **D-26**
    Mirasound 20.50.97 S
            Melomaan Ensemble, Hans Lamers, conductor

Evolutions (1958)   electronic ballet   **D-27**
    Limelight LS-86055

Figures sonores (1984)   **D-28**
    "Masterpieces for Band," vol. 4
    MBCD 31.1017.72
            Conservatorium Harmonieorkest, Maatstricht,
            Sef Pijpers, conductor

Finnegan's Wake (1978)   **D-29**
    Harmoniagram HG 3252 S
            Voorburg Jongerenkoor, Ad de Groot, conductor

Fünf Reich-Lieder (1974)   **D-30**
    MA 25015
            Helga Schulz and Hellmut Schoell

Genesis (1958)   electronic music   **D-31**
    Limelight LS-86055

Images (1983)   D-32
   Mirasound 20.50.97 S
      Fanfare St. Jozef, Meers, Hans Lamers, conductor

Kain and Abel (1956)   D-33
   "Anthology of Dutch Electronic Tape Music"
   Donemus/CV 7803; Philips 400063AE 45t
      Realized at the Studio Philips, Eindhoven

Kontrapunkte (1970)   for piano and electronic tape   D-34
   Marhel MA 25007 S
      Hellmut Schoell, piano

Het lied van Piet Hein (1963)   D-35
   Philvox XLP 050582
      Nachtegaal Mannerkoor Someren, Harris Swinkels,
         conductor

Lieshout en zijn molens (1976)   D-36
   Eurosound ES 46.564 S
      Fanfare "St. Cecilia," America, Leon Adams,
         conductor

Lieshout en zijn molens (1976)   D-37
   Eurosound ES 46.315 S
      Harmonie Excelsior Gemert, Berry van Oort,
         conductor

La malinconia (1949)   D-38
   Dimension D5631 S
      The Bilger Duo, David Bilger, alto saxophone;
         Dorinne Bilger, piano; with works by Eugene
         Bozza, Joseph Hector Fiocco, George Frideric
         Handel, Walter S. Hartley, Erwin Chandler,
         and Henry Cowell

La malinconia (1949)   D-39
   Col Legno CD 0647 238 (recorded 18-20 December 1987)
      John-Edward Kelly, alto saxophone; Bob Versteegh,
         piano; with works by Maurice Karkoff, Milos
         Maros, Werner Wolf Glaser, Otmar Macha,
         and Ernst Lothar von Knorr

La malinconia   (1949)   D-40
  "Vintage of European Saxophone Music," vol. 1
  8849 Fidelio
       Hans deJong, saxophone; Paul Hermsen, piano

Merck toch hoe sterck   (1978)   D-41
  Harmoniagram HG 3252 S
       Voorburg Jongerenkoor, Ad de Groot, conductor

Nu syt wellecome   (1950)   D-42
  (arranged by Badings)
  Larigot CD LAR 803
       Aalsmeer Jeugdkoor, Yvonne Keizer, conductor

Nu syt wellecome   (1950)   D-43
  Harmoniagram HG 3253 S
       "Arti Vocali," Hans Kronenburg, conductor

Octet   (1952)   Scherzo   D-44
  Radio Nederland AA 109021.2R/109022.2R
       Amsterdam Chamber Music Society

Octet   (1952)   D-45
  Decca London SSD 315 S
       Vienna Octet

Passacaglia   (1958)   for organ and timpani   D-46
  Lyrichord 7221
       Wendell Piehler, playing the Woolsey Hall organ,
         Yale University

Pittsburgh Concerto   (1965)   D-47
  AWS SR4s 3263 S
       American Wind Symphony Orchestra, Robert
         Boudreau, conductor

Quaderni sonori   (1976)   D-48
  Marhel MA 25026 S
       Helmut Schoell, piano

Quadruple-Concerto for Four Saxophones   (1984)   D-49
  Voor Saxofoonkwartet en Blaasorkest; Mirasound 49.9025 CD
       Brabant Saxofoonkwartet; Brabant Conservatorium
         Harmonieorkest, Jan Cober, conductor

Reflections (1980)   **D-50**
    Crest Records D-81-ABA (recorded 4-5 and 7 March 1981)
        United States Air Force Band, Arnald D. Gabriel,
            conductor; with works by John Philip Sousa,
            Paul Creston, Harold Walters, Frank W.
            Erickson, Alberto Ginastera, James Barnes,
            and William Schuman

Reflections (1980)   **D-51**
    Premiere 40640/United States Air Force Band (1-2 June 1982)
        United States Air Force Band, Arnald D. Gabriel,
            conductor; with works by Claude Smith and
            Vaclav Nelhybel

Reflections (1980)   **D-52**
    (Impressions, Interplay, Evolutions)
    Silver Crest MID-81-5
        United States Air Force Band and Singing Sergeants,
            Arnald D. Gabriel, conductor; with works by
            Jacques Offenbach, Kenneth J. Alford, Claude
            Smith, Roger Nixon, Vaclav Nelhybel, Maurice
            Ravel, and George M. Cohan

Reflections (1980) for wind orchestra   **D-53**
    Mirasound 49.9025 CD
        Brabant Conservatorium Harmonieorkest, Jan
            Cober, conductor

Reihe kleiner Klangstücke (1957)   **D-54**
    Sarabande, Recitativo, Pastorale
    Teylers Museum RC 227 S
        Anton de Beer, organ

Roemeense reisschetsen (1935)   **D-55**
    (Romanian Traveling Sketches)
    Marhel MA 25033 S
        Hellmut Schoell, piano

Sechs Lechler-Lieder (1966)   **D-56**
    MA 25015
        Helga Schulz and Hellmut Schoell

Sinfonietta 2 (1981)   **D-57**
    Mirasound 49.9025 CD
        Brabant Conservatorium Harmonieorkest, Jan
            Cober, conductor

Sonata 1 (1934) for piano   **D-58**
   MA 25007
      Hellmut Schoell

Sonata 2 (1941) for piano   **D-59**
   MA 30019
      Hellmut Schoell

Sonata 3 (1944) for piano   **D-60**
   MA 30019
      Hellmut Schoell

Sonata 4 (1945) for piano   **D-61**
   MA 25008
      Hellmut Schoell

Sonata 5 (1945) for piano   **D-62**
   MA 25008
      Hellmut Schoell

Sonata 6 (1947) for piano   **D-63**
   MA 30019
      Hellmut Schoell

Sonata (1957) for recorder and harpsichord   **D-64**
   Decca 93502 S
      Kirsten Behrman, recorder; Rita Laugs, harpsichord

Sonata 1 (1928) for two violins   **D-65**
   Marhel MA 30032 S
      Jeanne Vos and Bouw Lemkes

Sonata 2 (1963) for two violins   **D-66**
   Marhel MA 30032 S
      Jeanne Vos and Bouw Lemkes

Sonata 3 (1967) for two violins   **D-67**
   Marhel MA 30032 S
      Jeanne Vos and Bouw Lemkes

Sonata 3 (1967) for two violins   **D-68**
   Teylers Museum RC 227
      Jeanne Vos and Bouw Lemkes

Sonata 4   (1975)   for two violins   **D-69**
  Marhel MA 30032 S
        Jeanne Vos and Bouw Lemkes

Sonata 1   (1933)   for violin and piano   **D-70**
  MA 30012
        Harold Kalafusz and Hellmut Schoell

Sonata 2   (1939)   for violin and piano   **D-71**
  MA 25010
        Harold Kalafusz and Hellmut Schoell

Sonata 3   (1952)   for violin and piano   **D-72**
  MA 30012
        Harold Kalafusz and Hellmut Schoell

Sonata 4   (1931)   for violin and piano   **D-73**
  MA 25010
        Harold Kalafusz and Hellmut Schoell

Sonata 3   (1951)   for violin   **D-74**
  Orion ORS 78293
        Michael Davis; with works by Sergei Prokofiev,
            Sir Lennox Berkeley, and Paul Ben-Haim

Sonata 2   (1951)   for violoncello   **D-75**
  Donemus DAVS 6102 M
        Anner Bijlsma

Sonata 2   (1934)   for violoncello and piano   **D-76**
  SM 30 cm, Corona 30017
        Bielefelder Duo

String Quartet 3   (1944)   **D-77**
  Alpha DBM-V 166 S
        Dékány Quartet

Suite   (1954)   for 31-tone organ   **D-78**
  Philips 400090AE
        Anton de Beer

Suite 1   (1943)   for carillon   **D-79**
  Donemus DISK 001
        Jacques Maassen on the carillon of the Great Church,
            Breda; with works by Willem Pijper, Albert de
            Klerk, Leen't Hart, Wim Franken, Daan
            Manneke

Symphony 3 (1934)   **D-80**
"Highlights of the 1930-1950 Dutch Orchestral Repertoire"
Composers' Voice CV 8303
        Concertgebouw Orchestra of Amsterdam; Willem
          van Otterloo, conductor; with works by Henrik
          Andriessen, Sem Dresden, Hans Henkmans,
          Leon Orthel, and Willem Pijper

Symphony 7 (1954)   **D-81**
LOU 56-6 M
        Louisville Symphony, Robert Whitney, conductor

Symphony 8 (1956)   **D-82**
Donemus DAVS 6303 M
        Utrecht Philharmonic Orchestra, Paul Hupperts,
          conductor

Symphony 9 (1960) for string orchestra   **D-83**
Donemus DAVS 6602 M
        Netherlands Chamber Orchestra, David Zinman,
          conductor

Symphony 15 "Conflicts and Confluences" (1983)   **D-84**
"Chanson de matin"
MBCD 31.1006.72
        Maastricht Harmonie Orkest, Sef Pijpers, conductor

Symphony 15 "Conflicts and Confluences" (1983)   **D-85**
"Aspects of Wind Music from the Netherlands"
BFO A9 CD
        Nationaal Jeugd Harmonie Orkest (Dutch), Jan
          Cober, conductor

Tema con variazioni (1938)   **D-86**
Marhel MA 25033 S
        Hellmut Schoell, piano

Transitions (1973)   **D-87**
Silver Crest CBDNA-73-8
        Harry Begian, conductor; with works by Zoltan
          Kodaly, Richard Strauss, Paul Creston, Arnold
          Schoenberg, Ottorino Respighi, and John Philip
          Sousa

Trois Chansons bretonnes   (1946)   **D-88**
> EMI 153-29916/19 S
>> K. Hindart, piano; Stockholmer Kammerchor; Eric
>> Ericson, conductor; with works by Claude
>> Debussy, Maurice Ravel, and Francis Poulenc

Vijf Nederlandse dansen   (1976)   **D-89**
> (Five Dutch Dances, Suite 2)
> Harmoniagram HG 3000 S
>> Jeugd en Muziek Regionaal Jeugdorkest Noord-Oost,
>> Ru Sevenhuysen, conductor

Voici le bois   (1978)   **D-90**
> Mirasound KS 7039 S
>> Sint Maartenscollege Schoolkoor, Voorburg,
>> Ad de Groot, conductor

Des winters als het regent   (1950)   **D-91**
> Harmoniagram HG 2999 S
>> Arti Vocali; Hans Kronenburg, conductor

ARTICLES BY HENK BADINGS
(IN CHRONOLOGICAL ORDER)

ENGLISH

"Electronic Music: Its Development in the Netherlands." *Delta* 4 (1958-59): 85-93.

"The International Conference of Composers at the Stratford Festival, Canada, 1960." *Musical Events* 15 (February 1960): 44.
> A review of the conference. The Netherlands was represented by Badings's *Capriccio* for violin and electronic music and *Genesis* for five sinewave generators.

"Sonata for Cello Solo." *Sonorum speculum* 7 (June 1961): 23-24.
> An analytical discussion of the composer's Sonata 2

"Experiences with Electronic Ballet Music." *The Modern Composer and His World*, 106-08. University of Toronto Press, 1961.

"Composers' Corner (Composite Picture of What Dutch Artists Think about Electronics)." *Key Notes* 8 (1978): 56.
> Quote from Badings, talking about his penchant for acoustics and that tape recorders have helped him realize his dreams for composition with synthetic sound.

"Musical Perception." *Academiae analecta* (Academie voor Wetenshappen Letteren en schone kunsten van België) 48/1 (1987): 13-34.

FRENCH

"Sur les possibilités et les limitations de la musique électronique." *Revue belge de musicologie* 13 (1959): 57-62.

GERMAN

"Kompositionen für Kinder." *Musik im Unterricht*, Jahrgang 44, Heft 9 (September 1953): 245-46.

"Spezielles Gesicht der Funkoper." *Neue Zeitschrift für Musik* 10 (October 1955): 15.

"Bühnenmusik." *"Dabei," Blätter der Kulturgemeinschaft des DGB* (Stuttgart), Jahrgang 9, Heft 9 (September 1967).

"Über die Perzeption von musikalischen Klängen." *"Dabei," Blätter der Kulturgemeinschaft des DGB* (Stuttgart), Jahrgang 11, Heft 2 (March 1969).

DUTCH

"De Muzikale geometrie van Ernst Toch." *De muziek*, May 1931, 352-56.

"De Hedendaagsche Nederlandsche muziek." *Bigot and van Rossum* (Amsterdam, 1936), 113.

"Heilige huisjes." *De wereld der muziek* 11/12 (1939): 273-77.

"Eenige indrukken van de volksmuziek in de Roemeensche Zuid-Karpaten." *Leven en werken*, Jaargang 4, no. 1 (January 1940): 16-26.

"De Ivoren toren van de componist." *De wereld der muziek* 1 (October 1940): 297-300.

"Over instrumentalieleer." *De wereld der muziek* 8 (1942): 232-36.

"Tonaliteitsproblemen in de nieuwe muziek." *Kon. Academie v. Wetensch., Letteren en Schone Kunsten van België* (1951), 3-21.

"Luchtfoto's van dominerend componist en zijn werk." [Paul Hindemith]. *Elseviers weekblad*, March 1952.

"Strijdlustige Hindemith bijt fel van zich af." *Elseviers weekblad*, March 1952.

"Nieuwe opera van Malipiero." *Elseviers weekblad*, September 1952.

"Om de nieuwe muziek." *Elseviers weekblad*, September 1952.

"Muziekfeest Donaueschingen." *Elseviers weekblad*, October 1952.

"De kerkmuziek à la mode." *Elseviers weekblad*, October 1952.

"Naar de concrete muziek." *Elseviers weekblad*, November 1952.

[Essays on music theory.] *Winkler prins encyclopedia* 14 (1952): 110-53.
Rhythme, metrum en tempo
Melodie
Contrapunt
Harmonie
Vormleer
Geluidsleer
Instrumentenkunde
Instrumentatielleer

"Dodekaphonie niet in Genua." *Elseviers weekblad*, March 1953.

"Festival van Oslo." *Elseviers weekblad*, June 1953.

"Arthur Meulemans." *Mens en melodie* 9 (April 1954): 109-12.

"Arthur Meulemans, Vlaamse Debussy." *Elseviers weekblad*, May 1954.

"Twintigste eeuwse muziek in Rome." *Het vaderland*, April 1954.

"De Muziek der 20ste eeuw." *N. R. C.*, April 1954.

"Muziek en techniek." *Nieuwe Haagsche courant*, January 1955.

"Holland festival." *Elseviers weekblad*, July 1955.

"Overzicht van de muziek in historiographische tabellen."
Elsevier, encyclopedie van de muziek 1 (1956): 28-47.

[Essays on music theory.] *Elsevier, encyclopedie van de muziek*
2 (1956): 20-64.
Melodie
Ritme en metrum
Tempo
Dynamiek
Contrapunt
Harmonie
Instrumentenleer
Instrumentatie

"Concrete, electronische en radiophonische muziek" (with A.
Brandon). *Radio-electronica*, Jaargang 4, no. 3 (March 1956):
144-52.

"Robert Schumann." *Nieuwe Rotterdamsche courant*, July 1956.

"Inleiding tot 'Contrasten.'" *Koor en kunstleven*, December 1956.

"Electronische muziek" (with J. W. de Bruyn). *Philips technisch
tijd-schrift* 19, no. 9 (1957): 269-79.

"Elektronische muziek." *IVIO* (Amsterdam, 1958), AO-reeks,
p. 16.

"Over de moderne symphonie." *Intermezzo*, 3e jaargang, no. 4
(December 1958).

"De Toekomst der muziek." *Elseviers weekblad*, December 1958.

"Het muzikale element in elektronische muziek." *Utrechtsch
nieuwsblad*, March 1959.

"Het modieuze element in de muziek." *Tijdschrift "Zien"* 1, no. 3 (April 1959).

"Elektronisch muziekfeest in Gravesano." *Utrechts nieuwsblad*, September 1959.

"Het vioolconcert." *Intermezzo*, 5e jaargang (January 1961).

"Wezen en mogelijkheden der elektronische muziek." *Het vaderland*, March 1961.

"Electronica en de componist." *Tijdschrift v. h. Ned. electronica-radiogenootschap* 38, nos. 2/3 (1973).

"31-toon-stemming." *Musica*, 56e jaargang (1977), no. 6: 3-11; no. 7/8: 7-11; no. 9: 9-11.

"Over tempo en toonduur." *Musica*, 56e jaargang (1977), no. 12: 13-18.

"Over instrumentatie voor Blaasorkest." *Musica*, 57e jaargang (1978), no. 6: 21-23; no. 7: 19-20.

"Aantekeningen over enige fundamentele elementen in de muziek." *Mens en melodie* 41 (September 1986): 380-88; (October 1986): 452-53; (November 1986): 503-09; (December 1986): 547-51.

"Over 31-toon-stemming." *Koninklijke Academie v. Wetenschappen, Letteren en Schone Kunsten van België* (1987).

BIBLIOGRAPHY

Acton, Charles. "Cork: New Choral Pieces." *Musical Times* 103
    (July 1962): 480.
        This review of four new choral pieces written for the
        1962 Cork festival includes a brief statement about
        Badings's *Evocations*: ". . . analytically and on paper
        rather dull, *Evocations* showed itself in performance
        to have a strange excitement." **B-1**

Appleton, Jon. "Genesis." *Musical Quarterly* 55 (1969): 113.
        This review of the first performance of *Genesis* in the
        New Auditorium Maximum at the Technische Universität,
        Berlin, states that the piece was not well received. **B-2**

Baas, Beatrix. "Dutch 20th-Century Piano Music in Development."
    Key Notes 13 (1981): 28-37.
        This article discusses significant 20th-century Dutch
        composers, both teachers and students of Henk Badings.
        Sonatina (1950) is presented as a piece "very much
        worth playing." Other pieces mentioned are *Arcadia*,
        volumes 1-7, and *Concertino* (1967) for piano and
        electronic music. **B-3**

Baker's Biographical Dictionary of Musicians. 4th-8th eds. New
    York: G. Schirmer, 1940-92.
        A very brief but concise biography with a very accurate
        description of Badings's musical language. **B-4**

"Ballade, Symphonic Variations on 'There Were Two Royal   **B-5**
    Children.'" *Philadelphia Orchestra Program Notes*, 23 January
    1953, 427.

Becx, Caspar. "Henk Badings: Music for Wind-Orchestra."   **B-6**
    University of Utrecht, 1989.
            A complete thematic catalog of the music for wind
            orchestra. Written as a final project for a doctoral
            degree, the catalog includes a short biography, a
            historical perspective, background about the wind
            orchestra music, along with analyses of selected pieces.
            The body of the thematic catalog divides the works
            into four groups: 1) works for wind orchestra, 2) works
            for wind orchestra and solo instruments, 3) works
            for wind orchestra and electronic sound tracks, and
            4) works for wind orchestra and choir. A bibliography
            and discography conclude the catalog.

Broeckx, Jan. "The Apocalypse, for Chorus, Soloists, and   **B-7**
    Orchestra." *Musical Quarterly* 36 (April 1950): 286-87.
            Review of a performance of *The Apocalypse* on
            25 November 1949 in Rotterdam. "The evocation
            in this work is purely sensual, not plastic, and it
            seems to evolve essentially from an abstract type of
            lyricism joined with a kind of harmonization that
            makes extensive use of altered notes but is quite
            subtle in its resonance; at times the effect is very
            aerial."

_____. "Current Chronicle, Belgium and the Netherlands."   **B-8**
    Musical Quarterly 37 (July 1951): 420.
            Review of the premiere performance of *Symphonic
            Variations 2* ("Ballade, Variations on a Mediaeval
            Theme"). This positive article alludes to the freshness
            of Badings's "neatness and conciseness" seen during
            the fifties. The composer departs from the strict
            polyphony of earlier compositions to "an ample melodic
            outline, sustained by a moving harmonization."

Burde, Wolfgang. "Festwochen-konzerte: Woche der   **B-9**
    Experimentellen Musik." *Neue Zeitschrift für Musik* 129
    (December 1968): 509-10.
            The audience did not find favor in this performance
            of *Genesis* at the Fest-Week of Experimental Music

in Berlin. "Badings did not measure up at any moment, which is expected in the electronic medium, but carried on with unending broad and simple sounds."

Carl, Gene. "[Orestes] the Voice and Electronic Music." *Key Notes* 8 (1978): 28.   B-10

> This article makes very brief mention of the use of a male chorus recording played at double speed to raise the pitch an octave in the opera *Orestes*.

Clardy, Mary K. K. "Compositional Devices of Willem Pijper (1894-1947) and Henk Badings (1907-1987) in Two Selected Works: Pijper's 'Sonata per flauto e pianoforte' (1925) and Badings' 'Concerto for Flute and Wind Symphony Orchestra' (1963)." D.M.A. diss., University of North Texas, 1980. 49 pp. UM 81-09345. *Dissertation Abstracts International* 41A/11 (May 1981): 4534.   B-11

> The author examines Badings's *Concerto for Flute 2* (1963), giving special attention to form, tonal language, motivic material, orchestration, and new technical demands given to the soloist. The author concludes with a comparison of the two concertos and how Pijper may have influenced Badings.

Cohn, Arthur. "New York." *Music Magazine* 164 (May 1962): 25.   B-12

> A review of a performance of the *Double-Concerto 1* for two violins and orchestra by the Philadelphia Orchestra. First desk players Anshel Brusilow and David Madison were soloists. The piece is "second rate-up to date, modernized fiddle music."

"Composers of Recorder Music, Recorder Players, and Recorder Makers." *Recorder and Music Magazine* 7 (1983): 29-30.   B-13

> A very brief biographical sketch along with a notation of the three works Badings wrote for the recorder.

"Concerto for Two Violins." *Musical Opinion* 83 (April 1960): 455.   B-14

> A review of a concert given by the BBC Symphony Orchestra on 10 February 1960 under the direction of Rudolf Schwarz. Badings's *Double-Concerto 1* for two violins was given its English premiere by Alan Loveday and Hugh Bean. The reviewer is lukewarm in his acceptance of the piece.

Cox, Paul. "Guitar Music." *Notes* 30/4 (June 1974): 876-77.   **B-15**
  A review of *Twelve Preludes* for guitar. The
  reviewer points out that Badings wrote this piece
  from a technical point of view, with each movement
  presenting a different technical challenge to the
  guitarist.

Custer, Arthur. Review of Badings's "Concerto for Flute and   **B-16**
  Wind Symphony Orchestra." *Notes* 28/2 (December 1971): 305.
  The reviewer is disappointed in this second commission
  for the American Wind Symphony. He feels that the
  score needs much more substance to bring the music
  for this medium to a respectable level. Also the
  score and parts are in the composer's hand, making
  it extremely difficult to read.

De Beer, Anton. "The Development of 31-Tone Music."   **B-17**
  Sonorum speculum 38 (Spring 1969): 26-41.
  A comprehensive survey of the 31-tone system from its
  beginning with the 17th-century Dutch mathematician
  Christiaan Huygens to the present leader, Adriaan
  Fokker. Badings is cited as the first composer to
  write a full piece for the 31-tone organ at the Teylers
  museum in Haarlem.

De Beer, Roland. "An Odour of Taboo: Henk Badings,   **B-18**
  1907-1987." *Key Notes* 24 (1987): 28-29.
  A well written overview of Badings's career, with
  special attention to the less publicized "dark period"
  (1945-47) that resulted in his being barred from
  composing by the Dutch government.

De Rhen, Andrew. "American Waterways Wind Orchestra."   **B-19**
  High Fidelity/Musical America 20 (October 1970): MA-14.
  A disappointed reviewer talks about a performance
  of *Armegeddon* by the American Waterways Wind
  Orchestra on 26 July 1970 in Yonkers, N.Y. "Ambitiously
  conceived but unevenly executed, the music is best
  when it doesn't try too hard to make its point."

Dictionary of Contemporary Music. Ed. John Vinton. New   **B-20**
  York: E. P. Dutton and Company, 1971.

A very short biography citing Honegger, Milhaud, and Hindemith as influential colleagues. Also includes a list of principal compositions.

Ditto, John. "The Four Preludes and Fugues: the Ricercar and the Passacaglia for Timpani and Organ by Henk Badings." D.M.A. diss., University of Rochester, Eastman School of Music, 1979. 112 pp. UM 79-21120. *Dissertation Abstracts International* 40A/4 (October 1979): 2182. **B-21**

This dissertation concerns six organ compositions representing solo and organ with instruments. The author presents each composition from an analytical and musical point of view with the major thrust being a guidebook for performers. A short discussion concerning 31-tone organ compositions is also included.

Falk, Marguerite. "Henk Badings: 'Martin Korda D. P.'" *Schweiz Musik* 100 (1960): 375-76. **B-22**

A review of the premiere performance of *Martin Korda D. P.* at the Holland Festival in 1960. The production was a gigantic undertaking but not well received.

"First Performances." *World of Music* 10 (1968): 66. **B-23**

A review of the premiere performance of the *Concerto for Harp and Chamber Orchestra.*

Fokker, Adriaan D. "New Music and 31 Notes." Transl. by Leigh Gerdine. Bonn-Bad Godesberg: Verlag für systematische Musikwissenschaft, 1975. **B-24**

Geraedts, Jaap. "Symphony for String Orchestra." *Sonorum speculum* 6 (March 1961): 9-13. **B-25**

This analytical discussion of Badings's *Symphony 9* asserts that the players for this string symphony need to be able to play with a high degree of virtuosity.

Goldberg, Albert. "Novelties and a Birthday." *Musical America* 82 (July 1962): 13. **B-26**

A review of a performance of the *Double-Concerto 1* for two violins by Anshel Brusilow and David Madison of the Philadelphia Orchestra on 4 June 1962. The review describes the piece as a "serious and well wrought composition hovering between modernism and conservatism."

Goodfriend, James. "Philadelphia Orchestra." *Musical America*   **B-27**
82 (April 1962): 54.

> The reviewer gives a lukewarm response to the *Double-Concerto 1* for two violins performed by the Philadelphia Orchestra on 27 February 1962 in Carnegie Hall.

Griffiths, Paul. "Henk Badings." *The New Oxford Companion*   **B-28**
to Music, vol. 1. Oxford: Oxford University Press, 1983.

> A very brief biography.

Helm, Everett. "Dutch Music at the MIDEM Classique 1970."   **B-29**
Sonorum speculum 41 (Winter 1969): 24-26.

> A review of a performance of *Sonata 3* for two violins (31-tone) by the Duo Lemkes. The reviewer is quite taken by the legitimacy of the piece as music and not as a theoretical demonstration.

Hendrick, Herman. "Discriminatie van Badings." *Mens en*   **B-30**
melodie 38 (July 1983): 310-11.

> An article devoted to the awkward position that existed between the city of Eindhoven and Badings. Evidently there has been a strong political resistance to Badings's music in Eindhoven since World War II.

————. "Het scheppend jaar van een Nederlands Componist   **B-31**
met internationale uitstraling." *Mens en melodie* 39 (March
1984): 136-37.

> An article using the year of 1983 as an example of the amazing compositional output of Henk Badings. The composer made an effort to go to as many performances of his music as possible. Badings is quoted in the article: "I have never been afraid to write for performing musicians (amateurs and professionals). I want to create music which will give players and listeners pleasure."

"Henk Badings 80 Jaar." *Mens en melodie* 42 (January 1987): 15-17.   **B-32**

> A tribute to Henk Badings on his eightieth birthday. The article takes the eightieth year of his life as an example of the tireless energy that he has had for composing music. "Badings is an artisan of superb quality, who can produce usable practical music like few composers have. His music performs a social and pedagogical task." The article also reflects on

the consistent work it took to make a living as a
composer. "Badings has become one of the most
played and one of the most controversial Dutch
composers. That by itself gives him the right to
the respect he has received as a composer. The
controversy about Badings exists only in Holland."

Hill, Jackson. "Solo and Ensemble Music." *Notes* 29/4 (June   **B-33**
1973): 819-20.
> This article presents a review of *Sonata 3* for two violins
> (31-tone). After a brief discussion of the 31-tone
> system, the writer briefly discusses the piece and lauds
> the composer for his imagination and musical language.

International Who's Who in Music and Musicians Directory.   **B-34**
8th ed. Cambridge: Melrose Press, 1977.

Jaksic, Dura. "Opera na Holandskom Festivalu 1960." *Zvuk*   **B-35**
41 (1960): 87-92.

Kahmann, Ben. "Henk Badings en zijn geestelijke composities."   **B-36**
Gregoriusblad 113 (1989): 107.
> This article takes a close look at the sacred choral
> compositions of Badings. Frits Ham, of the Harmonia
> publishing company, says "it would be an exaggeration
> to say that choral music was the distinctive musical
> medium that he gave more attention. He also showed
> much interest and care for a healthy amateur music
> performance from which the professional side can
> develop." The author also asks the question why an
> unchurched man like Badings would devote so much
> time to sacred music. Badings relates "I was brought
> up in a free thinking minister's family. Through
> my mentor at the school in Delft, I became more
> informed about the Catholic faith. I have been
> appreciative of the aesthetic side of the liturgy which
> is the foundation for my religious compositions."

Kasander, John. "In Memoriam Henk Badings." *Mens en*   **B-37**
melodie 42 (July-August 1987): 322-27.
> A passionate account of the strong contributions that
> Henk Badings made to the world. A very personal
> description of the life of Badings and his thoughts as
> a composer.

Kellogg, Virginia K. "A New Repertoire: Music for Solo Violin **B-38**
and Tape." D.M.A. diss., University of Rochester, Eastman
School of Music, 1975. 112pp. UM 76-03689. *Dissertation
Abstracts International* 36/09 (March 1976): 5627.
> A discussion of four works for violin and tape written
> by 20th-century composers. Badings's *Capriccio* for
> violin and two sound tracks is presented in one of the
> chapters. The author includes a schematic diagram and
> discussion of the articulation of melodic material, the
> relationship of the violin and tape to each other, and the
> different technical demands placed upon the violinist.

Klemme, Paul. "Henk Badings: Choral Compositions for **B-39**
Unaccompanied Mixed Chorus with Latin Text: Analysis
and Commentary." D.M.A. diss., University of Washington,
1988. 238 pp. UM 88-26401. *Dissertation Abstracts
International* 50A/53 (August 1989): 294.
> This dissertation concerns five unaccompanied choral
> works written 1946-85, *Missa brevis* (1946), *Canamus
> amici* (1957), *Languentibus in purgatorio* (1959),
> *Querela pacis* (1979), *Missa Antiphonica* (1985). The
> author looks at each work from a conductor's view-
> point highlighting structural, stylistic, melodic, and
> harmonic features.

"Korda, Martin, D. P." *Rassegna musicale* 30 (1960): 266-67. **B-40**

Kox, Hans. "Symphony No. 8, D. A. V. – Series 1963/3." **B-41**
Sonorum speculum 16 (September 1963): 15-19.
> An analytical discussion of Badings's *Symphony 8*.

Lemkes, Bouw, and Jeanne Vos. *"Trio-Cosmos* van Henk **B-42**
Badings, voor groepsonderwijs vioolspel." *Mens en melodie*
38 (March 1983): 124-25.
> This review is the contribution of two violinists who
> played quite a lot of Badings's string music. "The
> composer takes into account the order in which the
> technique needs to be developed." Written with
> young players in mind, "this is a milestone in the
> violin literature for group instruction."

Libbert, Jürgen. "Gitarre und Orgel: Ein Beitrag zur Gitarren- **B-43**
Kammermusik" [Guitar and Organ: An Essay on Chamber
Music with Guitar]. *Zupfmusik-Gitarre* (Reutlingen) 31/3
(September 1978): 51-53.

Limmert, E. "Harlekinade und electronisches Ballett." [Die   **B-44**
Frau aus Andros.] *Musica* 14 (June 1960): 374-75.

MacDaniel, Charles. "Henk Badings: Musico-Technical Study of   **B-45**
his Woodwind Chamber Works." D.M.A. diss., University
of Texas, 1960.

Mitchell, Donald. "Some First Performances." *Musical Times*   **B-46**
94 (December 1953): 577.
> This review of Badings's *Sonata 3* for violin described
> the work as "banal, which progressed from one
> embarassing just-post-Brahmsian cliché to another."

_____. "Some First Performances." *Musical Times* 97 (April   **B-47**
1956): 205-06.
> This review blasts Badings's piano *Sonata 6* by first
> stating that so much of Dutch music today (1956) is
> "impressionist lyricism derived from French sources."
> The reviewer continues with "there are many passages in
> this sonata which could be demonstrated with reasonable
> objectivity as examples of inferior composition."
> Alexander Roediger was the soloist in this English
> premiere performance at London's Wigmore Hall on
> 23 February 1956.

Paap, Wouter. "Concert voor twee violen en orkest in de 31-   **B-48**
toonstemming van Henk Badings." *Mens en melodie* 25
(March 1970): 90-91.
> A detailed account of the compositional thought
> process that Badings encounters in writing music for
> 31-tone string combinations. "The accompaniment
> consists of a few chords against which the soloists
> respond."

_____. "Elektronische muziek." [Kain en Abel.] *Mens en*   **B-49**
melodie 2 (September 1956): 270-71.
> The article recognizes Badings as the leading Dutch
> composer of electronic music. The author also
> acknowledges the fact that Badings breaks the
> mold of the typical electronic music composer by
> generating pitch classes and using them in a traditional
> motivic manner. "Badings sees a new color that
> electronic music can give to the general overall
> musical language."

Payne, Anthony. "On the Right Track?" *Music and Musicians*   **B-50**
11 (July 1963): 10.
> A review of a performance of *Capriccio* for violin
> and sound tracks in London on 13 May 1963. The
> reviewer claims that piece bore the "closest resemblance
> to a conventional instrumental work." (Other works
> for instruments and tape were included on the program).
> He goes on to say "there was hardly a bar which I
> did not feel I could have made just as effective by
> scoring it for orchestra. Badings's work in spite of
> its electronic glamour, spoke the tired language of
> Romantic expressionism."

"Premieres." *BMI, MusicWorld* (October 1967): 21-22.   **B-51**
> Cites the premiere performance of the *Concerto for
> Harp* with Wind Orchestra on 18 June 1967 in
> Pittsburgh. Marcela Kozikova was the soloist.

"Premieres." *BMI: MusicWorld* (October 1969): 24.   **B-52**
> Cites the premiere performance of *Tower Music* by
> the American Wind Symphony, conducted by Robert
> Bodreau, on 13 July 1969 in Pittsburgh.

"Premieres." *Journal of the International Trombone Association*   **B-53**
15 (1987): 46.
> Cites the premiere performance of the *Concerto for
> Trombone* by trombonist Don Lucas and the American
> Wind Symphony Orchestra on 24 May 1987.

Rasincki, Jürgen. "Henk Badings: 'Tri-Cosmos' Spielmusik für   **B-54**
drei Violinen." *Üben and Musigieren* 4 (August 1984): 266-67.
> A review of the newly published *Trio Cosmos*, vols. 1-8,
> by Schott Music. The second set of eight volumes
> will be published soon. The reviewer praises the
> addition to the violin teaching literature. Special
> mention is made that one of the volumes is devoted
> to ornamentation.

Read, Gardner. "Armageddon, for Soprano Solo and Wind   **B-55**
Symphony Orchestra with Tape." *Notes* 26/3 (March 1970):
618-20.
> This review presents an excellent descriptive account
> of the score.

Ringer, Alexander. "William Pijper and the 'Netherlands School'   **B-56**
of the 20th Century." *Musical Quarterly* 41 (October 1955):
443-44.
> This article, devoted to William Pijper, mentions his
> students and their accomplishments. Badings's
> *Symphony 3* is mentioned as "almost old fashioned
> in the Brucknerian breadth of its phrases."

Rudd, Michael. "Stylistic Trends in Contemporary Organ Music.   **B-57**
A Formal and Stylistic Analysis of Post-World War II Works,
1945-1965." Ph.D. diss., Louisiana State University, 1967.
509 pp. UM 67-17343. *Dissertation Abstracts International*
28/07 (January 1968): 2719.
> A comprehensive survey of solo organ compositions
> written between 1945 and 1965 by composers from
> Europe and North America. The author divides the
> survey into three compositional categories: 1) neo-
> baroque; 2) neo-romantic; and 3) syncretistic. Under
> the neo-romantic heading the author discusses Badings's
> *Prelude and Fugue 4*.

Rutland, Harold. "Royal Philharmonic Society." *Musical Times*   **B-58**
101 (April 1960): 244.
> This review of the *Double-Concerto 1* for two violins
> acknowledges Badings's intimate knowledge of the violin.
> The concerto received an "excellent" performance.
> Soloists in this 10 February 1960 program with the
> BBC Symphony Orchestra were Alan Loveday and
> Hugh Bean.

Salzman, Eric. "Sine Waves, Closed Houses, Walled Gardens."   **B-59**
New York Times, 7 August 1960, section 2, p. 9.
> An interview with Badings while he was in New York
> during August of 1960. The interview specifically
> concentrated on the large amount of compositions
> with electronic music.

Samama, Leo. "Badings, Henk Herman." *Dizionario della*   **B-60**
musica e dei musicisti, ed. Alberto Basso, vol. 1: *Le*
biographie (1991), 272-73.

————. "Badings, Henk Herman." *Musik in Geschichte und*   **B-61**
Gegenwart. 2nd edition (in progress).

Samama, Leo. "Badings, Henk Herman." *The New Grove*   **B-62**
Dictionary of Opera* (1992).

————. *Zeventig jaar Nederlandse muziek, 1915-1985.*   **B-63**
Amsterdam: E. M. Querido, 1986.
> A comprehensive discussion (pp. 138-48) of Henk
> Badings's life and compositional language citing
> appropriate examples from every medium. The
> author uncovers previously unmentioned facts about
> the period during World War II (1941-45). A
> discography is included.

Searle, Humphrey, and Robert Layton. *Twentieth-Century*   **B-64**
Composers: Britain, Scandinavia, and the Netherlands.
London: Weidenfeld & Nicolson, 1972.
> This work includes a short biography of Badings
> and cites significant pieces that received awards.

Smith, Dorman H. Review of "St. Mark Passion, for Soloists,   **B-65**
Male Chorus, Orchestra." *Notes* 29/3 (March 1973): 561.
> This review states that the piece "combines the many
> elements of Badings' style in a very successful way."
> The reviewer is disappointed with the composer's single
> tempo for over three-quarters of the piece.

Standage, Jennifer. "Anglo-Dutch Chamber Concert in   **B-66**
Amsterdam." *Musical Opinion* 88 (August 1965): 662.
> A descriptive account of *Sonata 2* for two violins
> (31-tone), played at a concert of Dutch and English
> music sponsored by the Donemus Foundation in
> Amsterdam. Bouw Lemkes and Jeanne Vos were the
> soloists.

Stürzbecher, Ursula. "Werkstattgespräche mit Komponisten"   **B-67**
[Studio Conversations with Composers], 230. Köln: Gerig, 1971.

Thomas, Ernst. "Festival mit Mahler, Britten, Badings." *Neue*   **B-68**
Zeitschrift für Musik 121 (September 1960): 316-17.
> An unfavorable review of a performance of *Martin
> Korda D. P.* at the Holland Festival in 1960. "Badings
> does not possess the dramatic verve. The great scene
> with electronic music, which is supposed to reveal
> Korda's subconscious, is not prepared very well."

Tidemann, Harold. "Adelaide." *Canon* 16 (August 1962): 22. **B-69**
    A positive review of the Australian premiere performance
    of Badings's *Symphony 8*. The reviewer states that
    the symphony "has a dramatic, percussive opening,
    and the development is strong in both sinew and
    commanding orchestration. The symphony itself is
    comparatively short. It is vital, well-balanced and
    strong featured."

"Uraufführungen." *Das Orchester* 33 (May 1985): 508. **B-70**
    Notice of a performance of the *Triple-Concerto*
    No. 3 for Flute, Oboe, and Clarinet in 's-Hertogenbosch
    on 23 May 1985. Soloists were Frans van de Wiel
    (flute), Anne de Vries (oboe), and Arno van Houtert
    (clarinet) accompanied by the Brabants Orchestra,
    Ronald Zollman, conductor.

Van Ameringen, Sylvia. "Henk Badings." *Musica* 7 (October **B-71**
1953): 430-34.
    An overview of Badings's life and compositional
    language up to his 46th year. The author uses the
    four and two hand piano pieces *Arcadia* to illustrate
    elements of his compositional style. A significant
    part of the article is devoted to a discussion of the
    octatonic scale, which Badings judiciously used in
    many of his works.

Van Delden, Lex. "The 1966 Holland Festival." *Sonorum* **B-72**
speculum 28 (Autumn 1966): 28.
    A review of the premiere performance of Badings's
    Concerto for Viola on 12 July 1966. Joke Vermeulen
    was the soloist with the Dutch Chamber Orchestra
    under the direction of David Zinman at the Holland
    Festival in Rotterdam. The work is "elegaic and
    sometimes stern on the basis of a familiar idiom
    which received scarcely surprising injections by the
    incidental use of 31-tone tuning."

Vranken, Joseph. "Het 'Te Deum' van Henk Badings." *Euphonia* **B-73**
44 (1962): 5-6.
    A detailed analysis of the *Te Deum* for male chorus
    and orchestra. Dedicated to C. Receveur, the
    composition "accomplishes the sense of the text."

Werker, Gerard. "De 'Psalmensymphonie' van Henk Badings."   **B-74**
Mens en melodie 9 (February 1954): 39-41.
> Cites the premiere performance at the Holland
> Festival in 1953. The author continues with a
> thorough musical analysis of the piece.

————. "Iphigeneia in Taurië." *Mens en melodie* 6 (July   **B-75**
1951): 201-04.
> A detailed account of the origin of Euripides' tragedy
> and how it needs to be presented on the modern
> stage. In this production the stage manager came
> very close. "This performance had outstanding
> qualities, which will make it well worth recording
> in the history of Dutch theater."

Wouters, Jos. "Badings, Henk." *The New Grove Dictionary of*   **B-76**
Music and Musicians (1980).
> A sketchy biography outlining the works of Badings.
> The author mentions the three established compositional
> periods, and cites good examples from the operatic
> and instrumental works. Unfortunately, very little
> mention of any keyboard, chamber, or choral music.

————. "Composers' Gallery: Henk Badings." *Sonorum*   **B-77**
speculum 32 (Autumn 1967): 1-23.
> Written on the occasion of Badings's 60th birthday
> and his acceptance of the Johan Wagenaar Prize.
> This essay documents Badings's life from 1930 to
> 1967. Works given particular attention include
> *Symphonies 3* and *6*, *Orpheus and Eurydice*, *Ballade
> for Flute and Harp*, and the opera *Orestes*.

————. "Compositori olandesi d'oggi." *Musica d'oggi* 3   **B-78**
(May 1960): 211-12.

————. "Contemporary Music in the Netherlands." *Musical*   **B-79**
Opinion 88 (May 1965): 464-65.
> The author describes Badings as the "best known"
> contemporary Dutch composer. The article is a
> general overview of Badings's compositional output
> and life up to the time of his appointment at the
> Hochschule in Stuttgart.

_____. "Dutch Music in the 20th Century." *Musical Quarterly*   **B-80**
51 (1965): 103-04.
> A thorough essay of Badings's career, outlining the
> "three compositional periods" and citing Brahms,
> Reger, and Hindemith as direct forerunners to his
> compositional language.

_____. "Holländische Musik im Zwanzigsten Jahrhundert."   **B-81**
Österreichische Musikzeitschrift 19 (July 1964): 309-10.

_____. "Largo and Allegro." *Sonorum speculum* 6 (March   **B-82**
1961): 18-20.
> This article is an analytical discussion of Badings's
> *Largo and Allegro*. The reviewer puts the piece at
> the same level as *Symphony 3* and *Symphonic
> Variations 1*, which gave the composer considerable
> attention when they were premiered. The most
> remarkable aspects of this piece include "a strong
> melodic expression, a tightness of form and a great
> mastery of counterpoint, while from a harmonic
> point of view tonality is seldom completely discarded,
> in spite of the many bi- and poly-tonal elements."

_____. "Niederländische Musik im 20. Jahrhundert." *Musica*   **B-83**
15 (May-June 1961): 237-39.
> A well-written overview of Badings's life and compo-
> sitional accomplishments. "One can characterize his
> writings in the manner of Brahms, Reger, and
> Hindemith. He wrote outstanding works in every
> medium."

Zijlstra, Miep. "Tien jaar Nederlandse liedkunst." *Mens en*   **B-84**
melodie 29 (December 1974): 391-95.
> A comprehensive article citing significant art song
> compositions by Dutch composers from 1964 to 1974.
> Badings's *Eight Cummings Songs, Sechs Lechler-
> Lieder*, and *Fünf Reich-Lieder* are discussed.

APPENDIX 1:
EDUCATIONAL MUSIC

PIANO

Two Hands

for beginners	**Arcadia,** vols. 1, 2, 3, 6, 7	**W-3**
	Reihe kleiner Klavierstücke	
for advanced players	**Boogie Woogie**	**W-4**
	Sonata 3	**W-18**
	Sonata 4	**W-19**
	Sonata 5	**W-20**
	Sonatina 1	**W-22**
	Sonatina 2	**W-23**
	Sonatina 3	**W-24**
	Sonatina 4	**W-25**
	Xenie	**W-31**

Four Hands

for beginners	**Arcadia,** vols. 4 and 5	**W-3**
for advanced players	**Arcadia,** vol. 8	**W-3**

VIOLIN

Violin and Piano

for beginners	**The Fiddler and His Mate**	**W-53**

for advanced players	**Air triste**	**W-50**
	Cavatina	**W-52**
	Romance	**W-54**
	Rondino	**W-55**

Two Violins

for beginners	**Kleine Duetten**	**W-75**
	Quick Step	**W-77**

Violin and Recorder

for beginners	**Suite 2**	**W-78**

Three Violins

for beginners	**Trio 4**	**W-101**
	Trio Cosmos 1-7	**W-110**
for advanced players	**Trio Cosmos 8-14**	**W-110**
for semi-professional players	**Trios Cosmos 15-16**	**W-110**

Two Violins and Viola

for advanced players	**Trio 3**	**W-100**

Violin and Organ

for advanced players	**Intermezzo**	**W-481**
	Quempas	**W-484a**

VIOLA

Viola and Piano

for advanced players	**Cavatina**	**W-63**

Viola and Organ

for advanced players	**Quempas**	**W-484b**

FLUTE

Alto Flute and Harp

for advanced players	**Cavatina**	**W-92**

OBOE

Oboe and Piano
for advanced players   **Cavatina**   **W-69**

Oboe and Organ
for advanced players   **Canzona**   **W-476**

RECORDER

Two Recorders
for beginners   **Suite 1** and **3**   **W-94, 95**

Recorder and Violin
for beginners   **Suite 2**   **W-87**

Three Recorders
for advanced players   **Trio 8**   **W-105**

SAXOPHONE

Alto Saxophone and Piano
for advanced players   **Cavatina**   **W-71**

BRASS

Two Trumpets, French Horn
  and Trombone
for advanced players   **Brass Quartet**   **W-112**
                                     Drie Nederlandse dansen   **W-111**
                                       (Three Dutch Dances)

INSTRUMENTS AT PLEASURE

Quartets of Different
  Combinations
for advanced players   **1-8**   **W-115**

APPENDIX 2:
YOUTH AND AMATEUR
ORCHESTRA

APPENDIX 3:
ALPHABETICAL LIST
OF COMPOSITIONS

A moda Gellega	voice and orch	**W-537**
Les achalunés	film music	**W-522**
Ach Elslein, liebes Elselein	male choir	**W-359**
Ach nichts ist weit und breit	voice and orch	**W-538**
Ach Sorg du musst zurücke stahn	female choir	**W-310**
Adagio	pf	**W-1**
Adagio cantabile	pf	**W-2**
Addio la Caserma	voice and orch	**W-539**
Adios, Ene Maitia	voice and orch	**W-540**
Agnus Dei	female choir	**W-317**
Ain boer wol noar zien noaber tou	mixed choir	**W-261**
Ainhara	voice and orch	**W-541**
Air triste	vl and pf	**W-50**
Alle dinghe sijn mi te inghi	mixed choir	**W-262**
Als een goet instrument	declamatorio	**W-457**
An den Mond	alto and mixed ch	**W-263**
Apocalypse	mixed ch w/orch	**W-240**
Apparizioni	org	**W-464**
Arcadia	pf	**W-3**
Archifonica	org (31-tone)	**W-485**
Argizagi Ederra	voice and orch	**W-542**
Aria trista e Rondo giocoso	chamber orch	**W-136**
Ariettes méchantes, five songs	voice and pf	**W-416**
Ariosi e Fugati for fanfare orchestra	wind orch	**W-200**
Armageddon	wind orch	**W-201**
Asterion	opera	**W-501**

Au clair de la lune	female choir	W-318
Auf der Wiese	voice and orch	W-543
Auprès de ma blonde	male choir	W-360
Aus dem Ungarland	voice and orch	W-544
Aus tiefer Not schrei ich zu Dir	mixed choir	W-265
Ave Maria	female choir	W-319
Ave maris stella	female ch, orch	W-315
Ave maris stella	mixed choir	W-264
Ave Regina caelorum	male choir	W-361
L'Avvelenato	voice and orch	W-545
Azioni musicali	2 fl, 2 ob, 2 cl, 2 fag	W-128
Ballade	fl and arp	W-90
Ballade of Cocaine Lil	female choir	W-320
Ballade van de bloeddorstige jagter (Cantata 7)	mixed ch w/orch	W-245
Ballade van de omkransde boot	mixed choir	W-266
Ballade van de twee koningskinderen	female choir	W-321
Ballade van de watersnood	declamatorio	W-458
Ballade, Variations on a Mediaevel Theme (Symphonic Variations 2)	symphony orch	W-172
Balletto grottesco (two pianos)	pf / ballet	W-32
Balletto notturno (two pianos)	pf / ballet	W-33
Balletto serioso	symphony orch	W-157
Balletto serioso (two pianos)	pf	W-34
Beguine (four hands)	pf	W-35
Beguine	four treble inst., bass, perc, pf	W-129
Benedictus	female choir	W-322
La Bergère aux champs	male choir	W-362
Blues	harmonica	W-74
The Blue-Tail Fly	male choir	W-363
Bolke de Beer	incidental music	W-514
Boogie Woogie	pf	W-4
Burying Friends	voice and pf	W-417
Canamus amici	mixed choir	W-267
Canamus amici	female choir	W-323
Canarie	pf	W-5
Canon voor gelijke stemmen	male choir	W-364
Canso de Nadal	voice and orch	W-546
Canso de Sega (two versions)	voice and orch	W-547, 548
Cantata 1 *Festival Cantata*	mixed ch w/orch	W-241

Cantata 2 *Honestum petimus usque*	mixed ch w/orch	W-242
Cantata 3	mixed, childrens, male female ch w/wind orch	W-254
Cantata 4	mixed ch w/orch	W-243
Cantata 5 *Laus pacis*	male ch w/wind orch	W-355
Cantata 6 *Laus stultitiae*	mixed ch w/orch	W-244
Cantata 7 *Ballade van de bloeddorstige Jagter*	mixed ch w/orch	W-245
Cantata 8 *Song of Myself*	mixed ch w/wind orch	W-255
Cantata 9 *Christiaan Huygens Cantata*	mixed ch w/orch	W-246
Canzona	ob and org	W-476
Canzona	cor and org	W-477
Canzona	tr and org	W-478
Canzone di zampagnari	voice and orch	W-549
Capriccio	fl and pf	W-68
Capriccio	vl and pf	W-51
Capriccio	vl and tape	W-88
Carmina stultitiae	male choir	W-365
Cavatina	alto fl and arp	W-92
Cavatina	alto sax and pf	W-71
Cavatina	ob and pf	W-69
Cavatina	vl and pf	W-52
Cavatina	vla and pf	W-63
Chaconne	tr and tape	W-97
Chanson de Bourgogne en rondeau	male choir	W-366
Chansonnettes, six songs	voice and pf	W-418
Chansons orientales, four songs	voice and pf	W-419
Chorinus Kaiolan	voice and orch	W-550
Christiaan Huygens Cantata (Cantata 9)	mixed ch w/orch	W-246
Ciacona concertante	wind orch	W-202
Ciacona seria (brass band)	wind orch	W-203
Ciacona seria (Verses for Fanfare Orchestra)	wind orch	W-204
Cinq Poèmes chinois	mixed choir	W-268
Claghen	mixed choir	W-269
Concert Piece for Clarinet	cl and wind orch	W-227
Concertino	pf and el mus	W-38
Concerto for Clarinet	cl and wind orch	W-226
Concerto for English Horn *American Folksong Suite*	cor ingl and wind orch	W-228
Concerto for Flute 1	fl and orch	W-278

Concerto for Flute 2	fl and wind orch	W-229
Concerto for Harp	arp and orch	W-179
Concerto for Harp	arp and wind orch	W-230
Concerto for Orchestra	symphony orch	W-158
Concerto for Organ 1	org and orch	W-180
Concerto for Organ 2	org and orch	W-181
Concerto for Piano 1	pf and orch	W-182
Concerto for Piano 2 *Atlantic Dances*	pf and orch	W-183
Concerto for Saxophone	alto sax and orch	W-184
Concerto for Saxophone	alto sax and orch	W-231
Concerto for Trombone	trbn, wind orch	W-232
Concerto for Viola	vla and orch	W-185
Concerto for Violin 1	vl and orch	W-186
Concerto for Violin 2	vl and orch	W-187
Concerto for Violin 3	vl and orch	W-188
Concerto for Violin 4	vl and orch	W-189
Concerto for Violoncello 1	vlc and orch	W-190
Concerto for Violoncello 2	vlc and orch	W-191
Concerto for Violoncello 3	vlc and wind orch	W-233
Conflicts and Confluences (Symphony 15)	wind orch	W-222
Contrasten	mixed choir	W-270
Coplas	voice and pf	W-420
Coplas	voice and orch	W-449
Coucou, canari jaloux	voice and orch	W-551
The Countess Cathleen	incidental music	W-515
Cucu	voice and orch	W-552
Daar was een sneeuwwit vogeltje	female choir	W-324
Dance Variations (Symphonic Variations 3)	symphony orch	W-173
Danklied	voice and pf	W-421
Dialogues	fl and org	W-479
Dialogues for Man and Machine	el mus	W-530
Divertimento	symphony orch	W-159
Don Bosco cantate	male choir	W-367
Doodsbericht	mixed choir	W-271
Dormi, dormi bel Bambin	voice and orch	W-553
Double-Concerto 1 for Two Violins	2 vl and orch	W-192
Double-Concerto 2 for Bassoon and Contra-Bassoon	fg, c. fg and wind orch	W-234
Double-Concerto 3 for Two Pianos	2 pf and orch	W-193
Double-Concerto 4 for Violin and Viola	vl, vla and orch	W-194

Double-Concerto 5 for Two Violins	2 vl and orch	W-195
Drei geistliche Lieder auf altnieder-landischen Texten und Melodien	male choir	W-368
Drei Schwärmereien	mixed ch w/el mus	W-256
Drie baritonliederen	voice and pf	W-422
Drie duetten	sop, alto and pf	W-423
Drie duetten	sop, alto w/orch	W-446
Drie Dullaert-liederen for tenor	voice and pf	W-424
Drie geestelijke liederen	alto and org	W-454
Drie kerstliederen for soprano	voice and pf	W-425
Drie kerstliederen for soprano	voice and orch	W-450
Drie kleine klavierstukken	pf	W-6
Drie liederen op teksten van P. C. Boutens	male choir	W-370
Drie liederen van Minne	female choir	W-325
Drie mannenkoren op de teksten van de zuster van Gansoirde	male choir	W-371
Drie Nederlandse dansen	2 tr, cor, tbn	W-111
Drie Oud-Nederlandse liederen	voice, fl, arp	W-455
Drie Rilke-liederen	voice and pf	W-426
De driekusman	male choir	W-369
Een kindelijn zo lovelijk	mixed ch w/orch	W-247
Een klein weemoedig lied	male choir	W-373
Een meisje dat van Scheveningen kwam	male choir	W-374
Een oudt liedeken	mixed choir	W-272
De eendracht van het land	male choir	W-372
Eight Cummings Songs	voice and pf	W-427
Eine schöne gibt es nur	voice and orch	W-554
El pano moruno	voice and orch	W-555
Electro-magnetic Sound Figures	el mus	W-531
Les Elfes	declamatorio	W-459
En 's avonds	male choir	W-375
En passant par la Lorraine	voice and orch	W-556
Epiphany *I tre re*	wind orch	W-205
Es ist ein Ros entsprungen	female choir	W-326
Etude for Alternating Hands	carillon	W-490
Etude with Arpeggios	carillon	W-491
Evocations	mixed choir	W-273
Evolutions	ballet w/el mus	W-507
Fanfare de Jeanne d'Arc	symphony orch	W-160
Fanfare for 4 Trumpets	4 tr and orch	W-196
Festival Cantata (Cantata 1)	mixed ch w/orch	W-241

Feuillage du coeur	female choir	W-327
The Fiddler and His Mate	vl and pf	W-53
Figures sonores	wind orch	W-206
La filadora	voice and orch	W-557
Finnigan's Wake	mixed choir	W-274
Fisches Nachtgesang	mixed choir	W-275
Flog eine Falke	voice and orch	W-558
The Flying Dutchman	film, el mus	W-523
Foxtrot	pf	W-36
Fuga	fl, ob, vl, vla, org	W-480
Fünf kleine Klavierstücke	pf	W-7
Fünf Reich-Lieder	voice and pf	W-428
Fünf Rilke-Lieder	voice and pf	W-429
Gebed (Almachtige Godt)	male choir	W-376
Gedenckclanck	symphony orch	W-161
Gekwetst ben ik van binnen	voice and orch	W-447
Geluid van de werkelijkheid	declamatorio	W-460
Gelukwens aan Jos Vranken sr.	male choir	W-377
Gelukwenscanon	female choir	W-328
Genesis	ballet w/el mus	W-508
Genesis	male choir, perc, tape	W-357
Gentil coqu'licot	voice and orch	W-559
Gij volckeren hoort aen!	male choir	W-378
Gijsbreght van Aemstel	incidental mus	W-516
Goeden avond	male choir	W-379
Golden Age	wind orch	W-207
Greensleeves	wind orch	W-208
Gruselett	male choir	W-380
Had ick vloghelen als een arend grijs	mixed choir	W-276
Hannover Symphony (Symphony 8)	symphony orch	W-151
Harpsichord Concerto in A of J. S. Bach	harps and wind orch	W-235
Heer Jezus heeft een hofken	mixed ch w/orch	W-248
Hei, hier ein Hain	voice and orch	W-560
The Heroic Overture (Overture 2)	symphony orch	W-165
Herr Jesu deine Angst und Pein	mixed choir	W-277
Het daghet uyt den oosten	male choir	W-381
Het lied van Isabella	female choir	W-329
Het lied van Piet Hein	male choir	W-382
Hier is onze fiere pinksterbloem	mixed ch, orch	W-249
Hoe rij die boere	male choir	W-383

Hoelloch	film music	W-524
Holland Festival Overture (Overture 5)	symphony orch	W-168
Holland Rhapsody	symphony orch	W-162
Honestum pestimus usque (Cantata 2)	mixed ch w/orch	W-242
De hoorschelp	el mus	W-532
Hora	chamber orch	W-137
Huwelijkslied	mixed ch w/org (ad lib)	W-278
Huygens Suite	chamber orch	W-138
I Am a Poor Wayfaring Stranger	female choir	W-330
I tre re	voice and orch	W-561
Ich hab mei Muetli fast alles verloren	voice and orch	W-562
Ick sagh mijn nimphe	mixed choir	W-279
Ifigeneia in Taurië	incidental music	W-517
Ik weet nu zet uw shone deemoed in	mixed choir	W-280
Im Oberland	voice and orch	W-563
Images de Noël	pf	W-8
Images for fanfare orchestra	wind orch	W-209
In dir ist Freude	mixed choir	W-281
In memoriam	male choir	W-384
In memoriam	male choir	W-385
Indifference	film music	W-525
Intermezzo	vl and org	W-481
Intrada	wind orch	W-210
Introduction, Chorale and Finale on "Morning Has Broken"	org	W-465
Introduction, Variations and Indonesian National Anthem	wind orch	W-211
Irish Overture (Overture 6)	symphony orch	W-169
's Isch Aeben a Mönch uf Aerde	voice and orch	W-564
It Is Dawning in the East	guit and org	W-482
Izar Ederra	voice and orch	W-565
Jagerslied	male choir	W-386
La Jardinière du roi	voice and orch	W-566
De Jasmin	voice and orch	W-567
Java en poèmes (Six Images)	mixed choir	W-282
Jean de Nivelle	voice and orch	W-568
Jonah	mixed ch w/orch	W-250
Jubelstadje	female choir	W-331
Jubilate Deo	male choir	W-387
Juche!	voice and orch	W-569
Jungle	ballet w/el mus	W-509

Kain	ballet w/el mus	**W-510**
Kehr ich Abends heim	voice and orch	**W-570**
Keiner auch nicht einer	voice and orch	**W-571**
Kerelslied	male choir	**W-388**
Kerstdeclamatorium	declamatorio	**W-461**
Klaagsang	mixed ch w/orch	**W-251**
Kleine Duetten	2 vl	**W-75**
Kleine Ode für Jan Ter Wey	mixed choir	**W-283**
Kleine Suite	2 vl	**W-76**
Des König's Abschied	voice and orch	**W-572**
Kontrapunkte	pf w/el mus	**W-39**
Koperkwartet (Brass Quartet)	2 tr, cor, trbn	**W-112**
Kyrie eleison	female choir	**W-332**
Kyrie incantationes et meditationes	female choir	**W-333**
Lanceloet	incidental music	**W-518**
Languentibus in purgatorio	mixed choir	**W-284**
Languentibus in purgatorio	male choir	**W-284a**
Largo cantabile	alto sax and pf	**W-73**
Largo und Allegro	string orch	**W-134**
Laus pacis (Cantata 5)	male ch and wind orch	**W-355**
Laus stultitiae (Cantata 6)	mixed ch w/orch	**W-244**
Le Corbeau et le renard	female choir	**W-334**
Lentemaan (Sextet 1)	alto, fl, cl, vl, vla, vlc	**W-131**
Lied des Galeersträflings	voice and orch	**W-573**
Lied op het ontzet van Leiden	mixed choir	**W-285**
Lied op het ontzet van Leiden	male choir	**W-390**
Liederen van de dood	voice and pf	**W-430**
Liederen van dood en leven	voice and orch	**W-451**
Liederenbundel	male choir	**W-389**
Liefde's listen en lagen	opera	**W-502**
Liefdeslied	male choir	**W-391**
Lieshout en zijn molens	wind orch	**W-212**
Dat liet van den Rhijnscen wijn	male choir	**W-392**
Dat liet van Alianora	voice and pf	**W-431**
Loch Lomond	male choir	**W-393**
Louisville Symphony (Symphony 7)	symphony orch	**W-150**
Los wie d'Vögel liebli singe	voice and orch	**W-574**
Lucebert-Liederen	male choir	**W-358**
Das Mädchen vom Amselfeld	voice and orch	**W-575**
Malborough s'en va	voice and orch	**W-576**
La malinconia	alto sax and pf	**W-72**
Marche des vagabonds	male choir	**W-394**

Maria	voice, mixed ch, fl, vlc	W-257
Maria ging zware van kinde	female choir	W-335
Maria wandelte	voice and orch	W-571
Marion et le dragon	voice and orch	W-578
Mars	symphony orch	W-163
Martin Korda D. P.	opera w/el mus	W-503
Mater cantans filio	female choir	W-336
La megicana	pf	W-9
Meine Geige	voice and orch	W-579
Meiregen (ten children's songs)	voice and pf	W-432
Merck toch hoe sterck	mixed choir	W-286
Minnedeuntje Love Song	voice and pf	W-433
Missa Antiphonica	mixed choir	W-287
Missa brevis	mixed choir	W-288
Monsieur vous êtes jeun homme	voice and orch	W-580
Morgens is den riep zo kold	voice and orch	W-452
Morgenstern-Lieder	vocal quartet and pf	W-434
Die Mühle im Schwarzwäldertal	voice and pf	W-435
Mutter	voice and orch	W-581
Nachtgesang	female choir	W-337
De nacht voor morgen	incidental w/el mus	W-519
De nachwacht	opera	W-504
Najaarsnacht	voice and pf	W-436
Nana	voice and orch	W-582
Nie war hoch am Himmel	voice and orch	W-583
Nieuwjaarscanon	mixed choir	W-289
Notturno	male choir	W-395
Notturno triste alla luna	mixed choir	W-290
Nun Adé	voice and orch	W-584
O Mistress Mine	mixed choir	W-291
Oboe Quartet	ob, ob. d'am, cor ingl, hph	W-113
Octet	cl, fag, cor, str 5	W-130
Ode	female choir	W-338
Ode aan Aphrodite	voice and pf	W-437
Ode aan Roeske	male choir	W-396
Old Dutch Christmas Carol	wind orch	W-213
Old English Love Song/Sweet Nymph	female choir	W-339
Oneindige canon	mixed choir	W-292
Ons ghenaket die avondster	voice and pf	W-438
Op het tweede gehoor	el mus	W-533

Orestes	opera w/el mus	**W-505**
Orpheus en Eurydice	ballet	**W-511**
Oude Ballade	mixed choir	**W-293**
Overture 1 *The Tragic*	symphony orch	**W-164**
Overture 2 *The Heroic*	symphony orch	**W-165**
Overture 3 *The Symphonic Overture*	symphony orch	**W-166**
Overture 4 *Symphonic Prologue*	symphony orch	**W-167**
Overture 5 *Holland Festival Overture*	symphony orch	**W-168**
Overture 6 *The Irish*	symphony orch	**W-169**
Partita bucolica	wind orchestra	**W-214**
Passacaglia	pf	**W-11**
Passacaglia	timp and org	**W-483**
Passacaglia on BESC	pf	**W-12**
Passacaglia piccola	org	**W-466**
Pastorale	female choir	**W-340**
Pedal Etude	carillon	**W-492**
Piano Quartet	vl, vla, vlc, pf	**W-114**
Pittsburgh Concerto	wind orch w/el mus	**W-215**
La ploma de Perdiu	voice and orch	**W-585**
Polly Picklenose	declamatorio	**W-462**
Polnischer Winter	male choir	**W-397**
Preambolo, Aria e Postludio	guit	**W-45**
Predilcova	chamber orch	**W-139**
Prelude	pf	**W-13**
Prelude and Arioso	org	**W-467**
Preludio e Arioso	carillon	**W-493**
Preludium	org	**W-468**
Preludium en Fuga 1	org (31-tone)	**W-486**
Preludium en Fuga 2	org	**W-469**
Preludium en Fuga 3	org	**W-470**
Preludium en Fuga 4	org (31-tone)	**W-487**
Preludium on B.A.C.H.	org	**W-471**
Presents al nino Jesus	voice and orch	**W-586**
Psalm 42	mixed choir	**W-294**
Psalm 147	mixed, childrens, chamber ch w/orch	**W-252**
Psalm 27	male choir	**W-398**
Psalm Symphony (Symphony 6)	symphony orch and mixed ch	**W-149**
Psaume 42	female choir	**W-341**
Psaume Huguenot (Psalm 51)	male choir	**W-399**
Pupazzetti azzurri	chamber orch	**W-140**

Quaderni sonori	pf	**W-10**
Quadruple Concerto for 4 Saxophones	4 sax and orch	**W-197**
Quadruple Concerto for 4 Saxophones	4 sax wind orch	**W-236**
Quattro cavai che Trottano	voice and orch	**W-587**
Quattro pezzi	org	**W-472**
Quempas	vl and org	**W-484**
Quempas	vla and org	**W-484a**
Querela pacis	mixed choir	**W-295**
Quick Step	2 vl	**W-77**
Quintet 1	fl, cl, vl, vla, vlc	**W-122**
Quintet 2	fl, ob, cl, fag, cor	**W-123**
Quintet 3 *Capriccio*	fl, vl, vla, vlc, arp	**W-124**
Quintet 4	fl, ob, cl, fag, cor	**W-125**
Quintet 5	pf, 2 vl, vla, vlc	**W-126**
Quintet 6	cl, vl, vcl, guit, arp	**W-127**
Rackoczi-Lied	voice and orch	**W-588**
Ragtime	wind orch	**W-216**
Reflections	wind orch	**W-217**
Reihe kleiner Klangstücke	org (31-tone)	**W-488**
Reihe kleiner Klavierstücke	pf	**W-14**
Requiem (Introitus)	mixed choir	**W-296**
Requiem (Tractus)	female choir	**W-342**
Rey van Gozewijn	mixed choir	**W-297**
Ricercare	org	**W-473**
Rielen	chamber orch	**W-141**
Rijck God, Wien sal ick claghen	mixed choir	**W-298**
Ritornello di Lavendaja Wasurouwenhive	voice and orch	**W-589**
Roemeense reisschetsen	pf	**W-15**
Romance	vl and pf	**W-54**
Rondino	vl and pf	**W-55**
Royal Fanfare	wind orch	**W-218**
Sag, wie kann	voice and orch	**W-590**
Sag, wohin du Reiter	voice and orch	**W-591**
Sagas	wind orch	**W-219**
St. Mark Passion	male choir, orch	**W-353**
Salto mortale	opera w/el mus	**W-506**
Sass einmal ein Häslein an dem Rain	voice and orch	**W-592**
Satire	mixed choir	**W-299**
Schimplied (Swijgt onbeschaemde al-berispers)	male choir	**W-400**

Der Schlitter eilt	voice and orch	W-593
Schon drei Jahre liege ich krank	voice and orch	W-594
Schwarze Äuglein	voice and orch	W-595
Sechs Lechler-Lieder	voice and pf	W-439
Secret Passion	film music	W-526
Seh ich dich mein Herzensliebchen	voice and orch	W-596
Serenade	symphony orch	W-170
Serenade	string orch	W-135
Seven Quartets for Instruments at Pleasure		W-115
Sextet 1 *Lentemaan*	alto, fl, cl, vl, vla, vlc	W-131
Sextet 2	fl, ob, cl, fag, cor, pf	W-132
Sextet 3	sop, fl, cl, vl, cb, guit	W-133
Sicut lilium	female choir	W-343
Sigmund Freud	film, el mus	W-527
Sinfonia giocosa (Symphony 11)	symphony orch	W-154
Sinfonietta 2	wind orch	W-220
Skolion van Seikilos	male choir	W-401
Slaet op den trommele	male choir	W-402
Son tre mesi, che il Soldato	voice and orch	W-597
Sonata 1927	vl and vlc	W-85
Sonata 1928	vl and pf	W-56
Sonata 1928	vl and vla	W-84
Sonata 1929	ob and pf	W-70
Sonata 1944	arp	W-47
Sonata 1951	vla and pf	W-64
Sonata 1957	fl and harps	W-93
Sonata 1981	accordion	W-49
Sonata 1982	fl and arp	W-91
Sonata 1983	fl and guit	W-89
Sonata 1 1928	2 vl	W-78
Sonata 1 1929	vlc and pf	W-65
Sonata 1 1933	vl and pf	W-57
Sonata 1 1934	pf	W-16
Sonata 1 1940	vl	W-40
Sonata 1 1941	vlc	W-43
Sonata 1 1949	carillon	W-494
Sonata 2 1934	vlc and pf	W-66
Sonata 2 1939	vl and pf	W-58
Sonata 2 1941	pf	W-17
Sonata 2 1950	carillon	W-495
Sonata 2 1951	vlc	W-44
Sonata 2 1951	vl	W-41

Sonata 2 1963	2 vl (31-tone)	W-79
Sonata 3 1944	pf	W-18
Sonata 3 1951	vl	W-42
Sonata 3 1952	vl and pf	W-59
Sonata 3 1967	2 vl (31-tone)	W-80
Sonata 4 1931	vl and pf	W-60
Sonata 4 1945	pf	W-19
Sonata 4 1975	2 vl (31-tone)	W-81
Sonata 5 1945	pf	W-20
Sonata 5 1981	2 vl (31-tone)	W-82
Sonata 5 1984	vl and pf	W-61
Sonata 6 1947	pf	W-21
Sonata 6 1984	2 vl (31-tone)	W-83
Sonatina 1955	el mus	W-534
Sonatina 1 1936	pf	W-22
Sonatina 2 1945	pf	W-23
Sonatina 3 1950	pf	W-24
Sonatina 4 1958	pf	W-25
The Song of Lovers	female choir	W-344
Song of Myself (Cantata 8)	mixed ch and wind orch	W-255
Sonnet van Petrarca	male choir	W-403
Sound and Image	film music	W-528
Spiel nur, o spiel	voice and orch	W-598
De spreekcel	incidental, el mus	W-520
Stabat Mater	female choir	W-345
String Quartet 1929		W-116
String Quartet 1 1931		W-117
String Quartet 2 1936		W-118
String Quartet 3 1944		W-119
String Quartet 4 1966		W-120
String Quartet 5 1980		W-121
Suite 1930	pf	W-26
Suite 1954	org (31-tone)	W-489
Suite 1 1943	carillon	W-496
Suite 1 1950	2 fl	W-94
Suite 2 1951	carillon	W-497
Suite 2 1957	vl and fl	W-87
Suite 2 1958	3 fl	W-96
Suite 3 1953	carillon	W-498
Suite 3 1958	2 fl	W-95
Suite 4 1953	carillon	W-499
Suite 5 1983	carillon	W-500
The Symphonic Overture	symphony orch	W-166
(Overture 3)		

Symphonic Prologue (Overture 4)	symphony orch	**W-167**
Symphonic Scherzo	symphony orch	**W-171**
Symphonic Sound Patterns (Symphony 12)	symphony orch	**W-155**
Symphonic Triptych (Symphony 14)	symphony orch	**W-156**
Symphonic Variations 1	symphony orch	**W-172**
Symphonic Variations 2 *Ballade, Variations on a Mediaeval Theme*	symphony orch	**W-173**
Symphonic Variations 3 *Dance Variations*	symphony orch	**W-174**
Symphonic Variations 4 *Variations on a South-African Theme*	symphony orch	**W-175**
Symphonietta	chamber orch	**W-143**
Symphony 1	chamber orch	**W-142**
Symphony 2	symphony orch	**W-145**
Symphony 3	symphony orch	**W-146**
Symphony 4	symphony orch	**W-147**
Symphony 5	symphony orch	**W-148**
Symphony 6 *Psalm Symphony*	symphony orch and mixed ch	**W-149**
Symphony 7 *Louisville Symphony*	symphony orch	**W-150**
Symphony 8 *Hannover Symphony*	symphony orch	**W-151**
Symphony 9	symphony orch or string orch	**W-152**
Symphony 10	symphony orch	**W-153**
Symphony 11 *Sinfonia giocosa*	symphony orch	**W-154**
Symphony 12 *Symphonic Sound Patterns*	symphony orch	**W-155**
Symphony 13	wind orch	**W-221**
Symphony 14 *Symphonic Triptych*	symphony orch	**W-156**
Symphony 15 *Conflicts and Confluences*	wind orch	**W-222**
Tarantella de la Bellona	voice and orch	**W-599**
Te Deum	male choir, orch	**W-354**
Tema con variazioni	pf	**W-27**
Ten Green Bottles	male choir	**W-404**
Three Apparitions of a Hymn	wind orch	**W-223**
Three Hymns	brass, timp, org	**W-258**
Three Psalms	brass, timp, org	**W-259**
Three Sacred Songs	alto, ob, org	**W-456**

Three Serious Songs	mixed choir	W-300
Toccata	org	W-474
Toccata	marimbaphone	W-48
Toccata 1	el mus	W-535
Toccata 2	el mus	W-536
Tower Music	wind orch	W-224
The Tragic Overture (Overture 1)	symphony orch	W-164
Transitions	wind orch	W-225
Trauer um die Jugend	voice and orch	W-600
Die Traurige Braut	voice and orch	W-601
Tria amoris carmina	female choir	W-346
Trio 1 1934	vl, vlc, pf	W-98
Trio 2 1943	ob, cl, fg	W-99
Trio 3 1945	2 vl, vla	W-100
Trio 4 1946	2 ob, cor ingl or 3 vl	W-101
Trio 5 1947	fl, vl, vla	W-102
Trio 6 1951	2 vl, pf	W-103
Trio 7 1953	2 vl, vla	W-104
Trio 8 1955	3 recorders	W-105
Trio 9 1962	fl, vla, guit	W-106
Trio 10 1977	alto fl, vla, arp	W-107
Trio 11 1981	2 vl, archiphone	W-108
Trio 12 1986	cl, cor ingl, fg	W-109
Trios Cosmos	3 vl	W-110
Triple-Concerto 1 for Violin, Violoncello and Piano	vl, vlc, pf, orch	W-198
Triple Concerto 2 for Three French Horns	3 cor, wind orch	W-237
Triple Concerto 3 for Flute, Oboe and Clarinet	fl, ob, cl, orch	W-199
Triple Concerto 3 for Flute, Oboe and Clarinet	fl, ob, cl, wind orch	W-238
Tristis est anima mea	mixed choir	W-301
Trois Ballades	female choir	W-347
Trois Chansons bretonnes	mixed ch w/pf	W-260
Trois Chansons d'amour	female choir	W-348
Trois Chants populaires (3 Noëls)	male choir	W-405
Trois Chants populaires	female choir	W-349
Trois Romances	male choir	W-406
Trompetstemming	male ch w/wind orch	W-356
Tronfølgern in Latin Amerika	film music	W-529
Turned On	incidental music	W-521
Twee Breman-liederen	voice and pf	W-440

Twee kerstliederen op 14de eeuwse teksten	male choir	W-407
Twee Vildrac-liederen	voice and pf	W-441
Twee visies op een gedicht	male choir	W-408
Twelve Preludes	guit	W-46
Twentse suite	accordion orch	W-239
Two Grotesken	2 pf	W-37
Two Whale Songs	voice and pf	W-442
Unterm Fenster	voice and orch	W-602
Der Untreue	voice and orch	W-603
Up i dee	male choir	W-409
La va in Filanda	voice and orch	W-604
Variations	vl and guit	W-86
Variations à la manière de . . .	pf	W-28
Variations électroniques	ballet, film mus	W-512
Variations on a Mediaeval Dutch Theme	org	W-475
Variations on a South-African Theme (Symphony Variations 4)	symphony orch	W-174
Vaste gezangen uit Nocturne 5	mixed choir	W-302
De vechter	mixed choir	W-303
Vier geestelijke liederen	female choir	W-350
Vier geestelijke liederen	mixed choir	W-304
Vier geestelijke liederen	male choir	W-411
Vier kerstliederen	male choir	W-412
Vier liedjies van weemoed	voice and pf	W-443
Vier Nederlandse dansen	symphony orch	W-176
Vier volksliederen	mixed choir	W-305
Vier volksliederen	mixed choir	W-306
Vier voordrachtstukken	vc and pf	W-67
Vier wereldlijke liederen	male choir	W-413
Vier weverkens	male choir	W-414
Vier wiegeliedjes	voice and pf	W-444
Vier wiegeliedjes	voice and string orch	W-448
Vijf kleine klavierstukken	pf	W-29
Vijf Nederlandse dansen	symphony orch	W-177
Vijfstemmige canon	mixed choir	W-307
't Vloog een klein wild vogelken	voice and orch	W-453
Vocalizzo Burlesco	mixed choir	W-308
Voici le bois	mixed choir	W-309
De vrouwenboom	male choir	W-410

Wach auf, meins Herzens schöne	mixed choir	W-310
Wals	pf	W-30
Der Wandrer	voice and orch	W-605
War ein schöner Bursche	voice and orch	W-606
Warum, Lena so stolz	voice and orch	W-607
Was braucht man auf ein'm Bauerndorf	male choir	W-415
Wasch in weisser Milch	voice and orch	W-608
Wasserlein, kalt wie Eis	voice and orch	W-609
Weer is de tuin van Hugten	mixed choir	W-311
De westenwind	declamatorio	W-463
Westfriese boeren dans	chamber orch	W-144
Wiegenlied	voice and orch	W-610
Die winter is vergangen	mixed ch w/orch	W-253
Des winters als het regent	mixed choir	W-312
With All Good Wishes	mixed choir	W-313
The Woman of Andros	ballet w/el mus	W-513
Xenie	pf	W-31
Xenie	vl and pf	W-62
Yvonne's wiegeliedje	voice and pf	W-445
Zes oude kerstliederen	female choir	W-351
Zigeunerlieder	voice and orch	W-611
De zoom	female choir	W-352
Zwei Chorlieder	mixed choir	W-314

APPENDIX 4:
CHRONOLOGICAL LIST
OF COMPOSITIONS

1924

Ons ghenaket die avonstar	voice and pf	**W-438**

1927

Sonata	vl and vlc	**W-85**
Two Grotesken	2 pf	**W-37**

1928

Sonata	vl and pf	**W-56**
String Quartet		**W-116**
Alle dinghe sijn mi te inghi	mixed choir	**W-262**
Quintet 1	fl, cl, vl, vla, vlc	**W-122**
Sonata 1	2 vl	**W-78**
Sonata	vl and vla	**W-84**
Concerto for Violin 1	vl and orch	**W-186**

1929

Sonata 1	vlc and pf	**W-65**
Sonata	ob and pf	**W-70**
Toccata	org	**W-474**
Quintet 2	fl, ob, cl, fag, cor	**W-123**
Dat liet van Alianora	voice and pf	**W-431**

1930

Claghen	mixed choir	**W-269**

1930 - (continued)

Doodsbericht	mixed choir	**W-271**
Ik weet nu zet uw schone deemoed in	mixed choir	**W-280**
Suite	pf	**W-26**
Concerto for Violoncello 1	vlc and orch	**W-190**

1931

Sonata 4	vl and pf	**W-60**
String Quartet 1		**W-119**
Sextet 1 *Lentemaan*	alto, fl, cl, vl, vla, vlc	**W-131**

1932

Drie Rilke-liederen	voice and pf	**W-426**
Symphony 1	chamber orch	**W-142**
Symphony 2	symphony orch	**W-145**

1933

Sonata 1	vl and pf	**W-57**
Jagerslied	male choir	**W-386**
Had ick vloghelen als een arend grijs	mixed choir	**W-276**

1934

Sonata 1	pf	**W-16**
Dat liet van den Rhijnscen wijn	male choir	**W-392**
Trio 1	vl, vlc, pf	**W-98**
Symphony 3	symphony orch	**W-146**
Sonata 2	vlc and pf	**W-66**

1935

Roemeense reisschetsen	pf	**W-15**
Hora	chamber orch	**W-137**
Concerto for Violin 2	vl and orch	**W-187**
Drie Dullaert-liederen	voice and pf	**W-424**
Largo und Allegro	string orch	**W-134**
Twee Vildrac-liederen	voice and pf	**W-441**
Predilcova	chamber orch	**W-139**

1936

String Quartet 2		**W-118**
Vier wiegeliedjes	voice and pf or strings	**W-444, 448**
Drie baritonliederen	voice and pf	**W-422**

Drie duetten	SA and pf or strings	**W-423, 446**
De westenwind	declamatorio	**W-436**
Capriccio	fl and pf	**W-68**
Quintet 3 *Capriccio*	fl, vl, vla, vlc, arp	**W-124**
Capriccio	vl and pf	**W-51**
Sonatina 1	pf	**W-22**
Vier geetelijke liederen	female choir	**W-350**
Cantata 1 *Festival Cantata*	mixed ch w/orch	**W-241**
Symphonic Variations 1	symphony orch	**W-171**

1937

Overture 1 *Tragic Overture*	symphony orch	**W-164**
Cantata 2 *Honestum petimus usque*	mixed ch w/orch	**W-242**
Gijsbreght van Amstel	incidental music	**W-516**
Overture 2 *Heroic Overture*	symphony orch	**W-165**
Rey van Gozewijn	mixed choir	**W-297**
Minnedeuntje	voice and pf	**W-433**

1938

Tema con variazoni	pf	**W-27**
Gedenckclanck	symphony orch	**W-161**
Als een goet instrument	declamatorio	**W-457**
Preludium	org	**W-468**
Canzona	ob and org	**W-476**
Fuga	fl, ob, vl, vla, org	**W-480**
Intermezzo	vl and org	**W-481**

1939

De vechter	mixed choir	**W-303**
Balletto grottesco	2 pf / ballet	**W-32**
Concerto for Piano 1	pf and orch	**W-182**
Concerto for Violoncello 2	vlc and orch	**W-191**
Sonata 2	vl and pf	**W-58**
Drie kerstliederen	voice w/orch	**W-425, 450**
Reihe kleiner Klavierstücke	pf	**W-14**

1940

Java en poèmes (Six Images)	mixed choir	**W-282**
Liederenbundel	male choir	**W-389**
Liederen van dood en leven	voice w/orch	**W-451**
Twee Breman-liederen	voice and pf	**W-440**
Sonata 1	vl	**W-40**
De eendracht van het land	male choir	**W-372**

1941

Orpheus en Eurydice	ballet	**W-511**
Sonata 2	pf	**W-17**
Sonata 1	vlc	**W-43**
Een klein weemoedig lied	male choir	**W-373**
Vier geestelijke liederen	mixed choir	**W-304**
Chansonnettes	voice and pf	**W-418**

1942

Overture 3 *Symphonic Overture*	symphony orch	**W-166**
Overture 4 *Symphonic Prologue*	symphony orch	**W-167**
Triple-Concerto 1	vl, vlc, pf and orch	**W-198**
Chansons orientales	voice and pf	**W-419**
De nachwacht	opera	**W-504**
Intrada	wind orch	**W-210**
Coplas	voice and pf or orch	**W-420, 449**

1943

Suite 1	carillon	**W-496**
Trio 2	ob, cl, fag	**W-99**
Symphony 4	symphony orch	**W-147**

1944

Concerto for Violin 3	vl and orch	**W-188**
Sonata 3	pf	**W-18**
Ariettes méchantes	voice and pf	**W-416**
String Quartet 3		**W-119**
Fanfare de Jeanne d'Arc	symphony orch	**W-160**
Fanfare for 4 Trumpets	4 tr, orchestra	**W-196**
Sonata	arp	**W-47**

1945

Sonata 4	pf	**W-19**
Arcadia 1	pf	**W-3a**
Arcadia 2	pf	**W-3b**
Arcadia 3	pf	**W-3c**
Arcadia 4	pf (four hands)	**W-3d**
Arcadia 5	pf (four hands)	**W-3e**
Liefde's listen en lagen	opera	**W-502**
Sonatina 2	pf	**W-23**
Sonata 5	pf	**W-20**
Trio 3	2 vl, vla	**W-100**
Kleine Duetten	2 vl	**W-75**
The Fiddler and His Mate	vl and pf	**W-53**

1946

Trio 4	2 ob, cor ingl or 3 vl	**W-101**
Trois Chansons bretonnes	mixed ch and pf	**W-260**
Missa brevis	mixed choir	**W-288**
Meiregen	voice and pf	**W-432**
Vier voordrachtstukken	vlc and pf	**W-67**
Liederen van de dood	voice and pf	**W-430**
Ode aan Roeske	male choir	**W-396**

1947

Concerto for Violin 4	vl and orch	**W-189**
Maria	voice, mixed ch, fl, vlc	**W-257**
Drie liederen op teksten van P. C. Boutens	male choir	**W-370**
Air triste	vl and pf	**W-50**
Koperkwartet	2 tr, cor, trbn	**W-112**
Drie mannenkoren op de teksten vande zuster van Gansoirde	male choir	**W-371**
Twee kerstliederen op 14de eeuwse teksten	male choir	**W-407**
Trio 5	fl, vl, vla	**W-102**
Sonata 6	pf	**W-21**
Don Bosco cantate	male choir	**W-367**
Vier volksliederen	mixed choir	**W-305**
Yvonne's wiegeliedje	voice and pf	**W-445**
In memoriam	male choir	**W-384**

1948

Vier volksliederen	mixed choir	**W-306**
Les Elfes	declamatorio	**W-459**
Quintet 4	fl, ob, cl, fag, cor	**W-125**
Aria trista e Rondo giocoso	fl, cl, arp, pf, str	**W-136**
Kleine Suite	2 vl	**W-76**
Apocalypse	mixed ch w/orch	**W-240**
Vier liedjes van weemoed	voice and pf	**W-443**

1949

La malinconia	alto sax and pf	**W-72**
Prelude	pf	**W-13**
Sonata 1	carillon	**W-494**
Symphony 5	symphony orch	**W-148**
Divertimento	symphony orch	**W-159**
Holland Rhapsody	symphony orch	**W-162**
Trio 4	3 vl	**W-101**

1950

Folksong Arrangements	voice w/orch	W-537-610
Drei geistliche Lieder auf altnieder-	male choir	W-368
landischen Texten und Melodien		
't Vloog een klein wild vogelken	alto, fl, orch	W-453
Des winters als het regent	mixed choir	W-312
Sonatina 3	pf	W-24
Suite 1	2 fl	W-94
Ballade	arp and fl	W-90
Sonata 2	carillon	W-495
Symphonic Variations 2 *Ballade,*	symphony orch	W-173
Variations on a Mediaevel Theme		
Drie Nederlandse dansen	2 tr, cor, trbn	W-111
Pupazzetti azzurri	chamber orch	W-140
Zes oude kerstliederen	female choir	W-351
Lanceloet	incidental music	W-518
Three Sacred Songs	alto, ob, org	W-456
Trois Ballades	female choir	W-347
Trois Romances	male choir	W-406
Trois Chants populaires	male choir	W-405

1951

Trio 6	2 vl, pf	W-103
Zigeunerlieder - Dvořák	voice w/orch	W-611
Ifigeneia in Taurië	incidental music	W-517
Concerto for Saxophone	sax w/wind or	W-184, 231
	symphony orch	
Sonata 2	vlc	W-44
Suite 2	carillon	W-497
Sonata 2	vl	W-41
Variations à la manière de . . .	pf	W-28
Sonata 3	vl	W-42
Drie kleine klavierstukken	pf	W-6
Sonata	vla and pf	W-64

1952

Sonata 3	vl and pf	W-59
Preludium en Fuga 1	org (also 31-tone)	W-486
Contrasten	mixed choir	W-270
Preludium en Fuga 2	org	W-469
Cavatina	alto fl and arp	W-92
Quintet 5	pf and str. quartet	W-126
Octet	cl, fag, cor, str. 5	W-130

Concerto for Organ 1	org and orch	**W-180**
Cavatina	vl and pf	**W-52**
Cavatina	ob and pf	**W-69**
Cavatina	vla and pf	**W-63**
Cavatina	alto sax and pf	**W-71**
In memoriam	male choir	**W-385**
Vier kerstliederen	male choir	**W-412**
Sextet 2	pf, fl, ob, cl, fag, cor	**W-132**
Kerstdeclamatorium	declamatorium	**W-461**
The Countess Cathleen	incidental music	**W-515**

1953

Ballade van de watersnood	declamatorio	**W-458**
Wals	pf	**W-30**
Serenade	symphony orch	**W-170**
Symphony 6 *Psalm Symphony*	mixed choir and symphony orch	**W-149**
Preludium en Fuga 3	org	**W-470**
Suite 3	carillon	**W-498**
Suite 4	carillon	**W-499**
Symphonic Scherzo	symphony orch	**W-171**
Drie geestelijke liederen	alto and org	**W-454**
Three Hymns	brass, timp, org	**W-258**
Three Psalms	brass, timp, org	**W-259**
Trois Chants populaires	female choir	**W-349**
Trio 7	2 vl, vla	**W-104**

1954

Stabat Mater	female choir	**W-345**
Vier geestelijke liederen	male choir	**W-411**
Preludium en Fuga 4	org (also 31-tone)	**W-487**
Suite 1954	org (31-tone)	**W-489**
Vier wereldlijke liederen	male choir	**W-413**
Cantata 3	mixed, childrens, female ch w/wind orch	**W-254**
Adagio	pf	**W-1**
Cantata 4	mixed ch w/orch	**W-243**
Double-Concerto 1 for Two Violins	2 vl and orch	**W-192**
Orestes	opera w/el mus	**W-505**
Overture 5 *Holland Festival Overture*	symphony orch	**W-168**
Symphony 8 *Louisville Symphony*	symphony orch	**W-150**

1955

Balletto serioso	2 pf	W-34, 157
Concerto for Piano 2 *Atlantic Dances*	pf and orch	W-183
Sonatina	el mus	W-534
Trio 8	2 fl, alto fl	W-105
Foxtrot	pf	W-36

1956

Cantata 5 *Laus pacis*	male choir w/wind orch	W-355
De nacht voor morgen	incidental mus w/el mus	W-519
Kain	ballet w/el mus	W-510
Symphonic Variations 3 *Dance Var.*	symphony orch	W-174
Concerto for Flute 1	fl and orch	W-178
Symphony 8 *Hannover Symphony*	symphony orch	W-151

1957

Blues	harmonica and pf	W-74
Sonata	fl and harpsichord	W-93
Suite 2	fl and vl	W-87
Vaste gezangen uit Nocturne 5	mixed choir	W-302
Reihe kleiner Klangstücke	org (31-tone)	W-488
Vier Nederlandse dansen	symphony orch	W-176
Bolke de Beer	incidental mus	W-514
The Flying Dutchman	film w/el mus	W-523
Canamus amici	mixed or female choir	W-267, 323
Romance	vl and pf	W-54
Mars	symphony orch	W-163
Variations électroniques	film music	W-512
Asterion	opera	W-501
Op het tweede gehoor	el mus	W-533

1958

Diaglogues for Man and Machine	el mus	W-530
De hoorschelp	el mus	W-532
Suite 2	3 fl	W-96
Suite 3	2 fl	W-95
Genesis	ballet w/el mus	W-508
Xenie	pf	W-31
Boogie Woogie	pf	W-4
Sonatina 4	pf	W-25
Passacaglia	org and timp	W-483
Geluid van de werkelijkheid	declamatorio w/el mus	W-460
Evolutions	ballet w/el mus	W-507

1959

The Woman of Andros	ballet w/el mus	**W-513**
Languentibus in purgatorio	mixed or male ch or male ch w/soloists	**W-284**
Salto mortale	opera w/el mus	**W-506**
Capriccio	vl and el mus	**W-88**
Electro-magnetic Sound Figures	el mus	**W-531**
De spreekcel	incidental mus	**W-520**
Psalm 147	childrens, female, chamber ch w/orch	**W-251**
Xenie	vl and pf	**W-62**
Jungle	ballet w/el mus	**W-509**

1960

Partita bucolica	wind orch	**W-214**
Martin Korda D. P.	opera	**W-503**
Psalm 42	mixed choir	**W-294**
Quick Step	2 vl	**W-77**
Rondino	vl and pf	**W-55**
Symphony 9	string orch or symphony orch	**W-152**
Symphonic Variations 4 *Variations on a South-African Theme*	symphony orch	**W-175**
Oneindige canon	mixed choir	**W-292**
Les achalunés	film music	**W-522**

1961

Huwelijkslied	mixed ch and org	**W-278**
Twelve Preludes	guit	**W-46**
Morgenstern-Lieder	vocal quar and pf	**W-434**
Cantata 6 *Laus stultitiae*	mixed ch and orch	**W-244**
Symphony 10	symphony orch	**W-153**
Overture 7 *The Irish*	symphony orch	**W-169**

1962

Te Deum	male ch and orch	**W-354**
Trio 9	fl, vla, guit	**W-106**
Evocations	mixed choir	**W-273**
Sigmund Freud	film, el mus	**W-527**

1963

Jonah	mixed ch w/orch	**W-250**
Het lied van Piet Hein	male choir	**W-382**

1963 - (*continued*)

Concerto for Flute 2	fl and wind orch	**W-229**
Lucebert-Liederen	male ch, el mus	**W-358**
Burying Friends	voice and pf	**W-417**
Sonata 2	2 vl (31-tone)	**W-79**

1964

Double Concerto 2 for Bassoon and Contra-Bassoon	fag, c. fg and wind orch	**W-234**
Double Concerto 3 for Two Pianos	2 pf and orch	**W-193**
Symphony 11 *Sinfonia giocosa*	symphony orch	**W-154**
Carmina stultitiae	male choir	**W-365**
Drei Schwärmereien	mixed ch, el mus	**W-256**
Toccata 1	el mus (2 tr)	**W-535**
Toccata 2	el mus (4 tr)	**W-536**
Symphony 12 *Symphonic Sound Patterns*	symphony orch	**W-155**
Secret Passion	film music	**W-526**

1965

Pittsburgh Concerto	wind orch w/el mus	**W-215**
Double-Concerto 4 for Violin and Viola	vl, vla, and orch	**W-194**
Een meisje dat van Scheveningen kwam	male choir	**W-374**
Eight Cummings Songs	voice and pf	**W-427**
Ave maris stella	female ch w/orch	**W-315**
Chaconne	trumpet and tape	**W-97**
Concerto for Viola	vla and orch	**W-185**
De driekusman	male choir	**W-369**
Sound and Image	film music	**W-528**

1966

Vier weverkens	male choir	**W-414**
Concerto for Organ 2	org and orch	**W-181**
Symphony 13	wind orch	**W-221**
With All Good Wishes	mixed choir	**W-313**
Sechs Lechler-Lieder	voice and pf	**W-439**
Marche des vagabonds	male choir	**W-394**
En's avonds	male choir	**W-375**
Loch Lomond	male choir	**W-393**
Up i dee	male choir	**W-409**
Auprès de ma blonde	male choir	**W-360**
Ten Green Bottles	male choir	**W-404**

String Quartet 4		W-120
Hoe rij die boere	male choir	W-383
Was braucht man auf ein'm Bauerndorf	male choir	W-415
Goeden avond	male choir	W-379
Hoelloch	film music	W-524
Tronfølgernin Latin Amerika	film music	W-529

1967

's Morgens is den riep zo kold	sop w/orch	W-452
Een kindelijn zo lovelijk	mixed ch w/orch	W-247
Heer Jezus heeft een hofken	sop mixed ch, orch	W-248
Drie Oud-Nederlandse liederen	sop, fl, arp	W-455
Concerto for Harp	arp and wind orch or symphony orch	W-179, 230
Gekwetst ben ik van binnen	voice w/str orch	W-447
Die winter is vergangen	mixed ch w/orch	W-253
Hier is onze fiere pinksterbloem	mixed ch w/orch	W-249
Genesis	male ch, perc, tape	W-357
Westfriese boeren dans	chamber orch	W-144
Rielen	chamber orch	W-141
It Is Dawning in the East	org and guit	W-482
Sonata 3	2 vl (31-tone)	W-80
Canzona	cor and org	W-477
Quempas	vl or vla and org	W-484
Vijf kleine klavierstukken	pf	W-29
Het daghet uyt den oosten	male choir	W-381
Dialogues	fl and org	W-479
Adagio cantabile	pf	W-2
Concertino	pf and el mus	W-38
Arcadia 6	pf	W-3f
Arcadia 7	pf	W-3g
Arcadia 8	pf (four hands)	W-3h

1968

Armageddon	wind orch	W-201
Symphony 14 *Symphonic Triptych*	symphony orch	W-156
Indifference	film music	W-525

1969

Double-Concerto 5 for Two Violins	2 vl and orch	W-195
Variations on a Mediaeval Dutch Theme	org	W-475
Tower Music	wind orch	W-224

1969 - (continued)

Polly Picklenose	declamatorio	**W-462**
Ragtime	wind orch	**W-216**

1970

Ode	2 female voices	**W-338**
Gelukwenscanon	female choir	**W-328**
Triple-Concerto 2 for Three French Horns	3 cor and wind orch	**W-237**
Greensleeves	wind orch	**W-208**
Cantata 7 *Ballade van de bloeddorstige jagter*	mixed ch w/orch	**W-245**
Klaagsang	mixed ch w/orch	**W-251**
Kontrapunkte	pf w/el mus	**W-39**
Old Dutch Christmas Carol	wind orch	**W-213**
Gelukwens aan Jos Vranken sr.	male choir	**W-377**
Danklied	voice and pf	**W-421**

1971

St. Mark Passion	male ch w/orch	**W-353**
Canzona	tr and org	**W-478**
Turned On	incidental mus	**W-521**
Symphonietta	chamber orch	**W-143**

1972

Transitions	wind orch	**W-225**
Weer is de tuin van Hugten . . .	mixed choir	**W-311**

1973

Vijfstemmige canon	mixed choir	**W-307**
Cinq poémes chinois	mixed choir	**W-268**
Toccata	marimbaphone	**W-48**
Cantata 8 *Song of Myself*	mixed ch and wind orch	**W-225**
Ricercare	org	**W-473**

1974

Piano Quartet	vl, vla, vlc, pf	**W-114**
Trompetstemming	male ch and wind orch	**W-356**
Canarie	pf	**W-5**
Fünf Reich-Lieder	voice and pf	**W-428**
Die Mühle im Schwarzwäldertal	voice and pf	**W-435**

1975

Balletto notturno	2 pf / ballet	**W-33**
Sonata 4	2 vl (31-tone)	**W-81**
Introduction, Chorale, and Finale on "Morning Has Broken"	org	**W-465**
Oboe Quartet *Variations on the Bluetail-fly*	ob, ob. d'am cor ingl, hph	**W-113**
Concerto for English Horn *American Folksong Suite*	cor ingl and wind orch	**W-228**

1976

Twentse suite	accordion orch	**W-239**
Archifonica	org (31-tone)	**W-485**
Vijf Nederlandse dansen	symphony orch	**W-177**
Lieshout en zijn molens	wind orch	**W-212**
Quaderni sonori	pf	**W-10**
Kleine Ode für Jan Ter Wey	mixed choir	**W-283**
Canon voor gelijke stemmen	male choir	**W-364**
Najaarsnacht	voice and pf	**W-436**

1977

Nieuwjaarscanon	mixed choir	**W-289**
Preludio e Arioso	carillon	**W-493**
Apparizioni	org	**W-464**
Zwei Chorlieder	mixed choir	**W-314**
Trio 10	vla, alto fl, arp	**W-107**
Gelukwenscanon	female choir	**W-328**

1978

Fünf Rilke-Lieder	voice and pf	**W-429**
Ciacona concertante	wind orch	**W-202**
Beguine	pf (four hands), for four treble instr., bass, perc, pf	**W-35, 129**
Daar was een sneeuwwit vogeltje	female choir	**W-324**
Le Corbeau et le renard	female choir	**W-334**
Ave Maria	female choir	**W-319**
Ballade of Cocaine Lil	female choir	**W-320**
Es ist ein Ros entsprungen	female choir	**W-326**
The Blue-Tail Fly	male choir	**W-363**
I Am a Poor Wayfaring Stranger	female choir	**W-330**
Ach Sorg du musst zürucke stahn	female choir	**W-316**

1978 - (continued)

Ach Elslein, liebes Elselein	male choir	W-359
Kerelslied	male choir	W-388
Wach auf, meins Herzens schöne	mixed choir	W-310
Notturno	male choir	W-395
Ave Regina caelorum	male choir	W-361
Aus tiefer Not schrei zu Dir	mixed choir	W-265
Sicut lilium	female choir	W-343
Feuillage du coeur	female choir	W-327
Fisches Nachtgesang	mixed choir	W-275
The Song of Lovers	female choir	W-344
Mater cantans filio	female choir	W-336
Merck toch hoe sterck	mixed choir	W-286
Herr Jesu deine Angst und Pein	mixed choir	W-277
Au clair de la lune	female choir	W-318
Psaume Huguenot (Psalm 51)	male choir	W-399
Psaume 42	female choir	W-341
Voici le bois	mixed choir	W-309
Notturno triste alla luna	mixed choir	W-290
Finnigan's Wake	mixed choir	W-274
Quartets for Instruments at Pleasure	quartet 2, 3	W-115b-c
Requiem (Introitus)	mixed choir	W-296
Requiem (Tractus)	female choir	W-342
Gruselett	male choir	W-380
Vocalizzo Burlesco	mixed choir	W-308
La megicana	pf	W-9
Slaet op den trommele	male choir	W-402
Gij volckeren hoort aen!	male choir	W-378
Schimplied (Swijgt onbeschaemde al-berispers)	male choir	W-400
Gebed (Almachtige Godt)	male choir	W-376

1979

Golden Age	wind orch	W-207
Concerto for Clarinet	cl and wind orch	W-226
Kyrie eleison	female choir	W-332
Quartets for Instruments at Pleasure	quartet 4	W-115d
In dir ist Freude	mixed choir	W-281
Oude Ballade	mixed choir	W-293
Ain boer wol noar zien noaber tou	mixed choir	W-261
Epiphany *I tre re*	wind orch	W-205
Lied op het ontzet van Leiden	mixed or male ch	W-285, 390
Ariosi e Fugati	wind orch	W-200

Passacaglia piccola	org	**W-466**
Querela pacis	mixed choir	**W-295**
Passacaglia	pf	**W-11**

1980

Quartets for Instruments at Pleasure	quartet 1, 5	**W-115a, e**
Concert Piece for Clarinet	cl and wind orch	**W-227**
Quattro pezzi	org	**W-472**
Two Whale Songs	voice and pf	**W-442**
Reflections	wind orch	**W-217**
String Quartet 5		**W-121**
Azioni musicali	2 fl, 2 cl, 2 ob, 2 fag, 2 tr, vlc, cb	**W-128**
Trios Cosmos (16 sets of trios)	amateur violin groups	**W-110**

1981

Sonata 5	2 vl (31-tone)	**W-82**
Trio 11	2 vl, archiphone	**W-108**
Royal Fanfare	wind orch	**W-218**
Sinfonietta 2	wind orch	**W-220**
Kyrie incantationes et meditationes	female choir	**W-333**
Quartets for Instruments at Pleasure	quartet 6	**W-115f**
Triple-Concerto 3 for Flute, Oboe and Clar.	fl, ob, cl, wind or symphony orch	**W-199, 238**
Sonata	accordion	**W-49**

1982

Jubilate Deo	male choir	**W-387**
Polnischer Winter	male choir	**W-397**
Sonnet van Petrarca	male choir	**W-403**
Chanson de Bourgogne en rondeau	male choir	**W-366**
Skolion van Seikilos	male choir	**W-401**
La Bergère aux champs	male choir	**W-362**
Passacaglia on BESC	pf	**W-12**
Benedictus	female choir	**W-322**
Agnus Dei	female choir	**W-317**
Sonata	arp and fl	**W-91**
Concerto for Orchestra	symphony orch	**W-158**
Images de Noël	pf	**W-8**
Quartets for Instruments at Pleasure	quartet 7	**W-115g**
Ode aan Aphrodite	voice and pf	**W-437**
Ciacona seria (brass band)	wind orch	**W-203**

1983

Ballade van de twee koningskinderen	female choir	**W-321**
Images	wind orch	**W-209**
Sonata	fl and guit	**W-89**
Suite 5	carillon	**W-500**
Drie liederen van Minne	female choir	**W-325**
Trois Chansons d'amour	female choir	**W-348**
Tria amoris carmina	female choir	**W-346**
Old English Love Song/Sweet Nymph	female choir	**W-339**
Three Serious Songs	mixed choir	**W-300**
Largo cantabile	alto sax and pf	**W-73**
Prelude and Arioso	org	**W-467**
Fünf kleine Klavierstücke	pf	**W-7**
Psalm 27	male choir	**W-398**
Symphony 15 *Conflicts and Confluences*	wind orch	**W-222**
Maria ging zware van kinde	female choir	**W-335**
Variations	vl and guit	**W-86**

1984

Sonata 6	2 vl (31-tone)	**W-83**
Three Apparitions of a Hymn	wind orch	**W-223**
Quadruple-Concerto for Four Saxophones	4 sax (2 atb), wind orch or symphony orch	**W-197, 236**
Figures sonores	wind orch	**W-206**
De vrouwenboom	male choir	**W-410**
Liefdeslied	male choir	**W-391**
Sonata 5	vl and pf	**W-61**
Sagas	wind orch	**W-219**

1985

Missa Antiphonica	mixed choir	**W-287**
Preludium on B.A.C.H.	org	**W-471**
Concerto for Violoncello 3	vlc and wind orch	**W-233**
Twee visies op een gedicht	male choir	**W-408**
Preambolo, Aria e Postludio	guit	**W-45**
Pck sagh mijn nimphe	mixed choir	**W-279**
Rijck God, Wien sal ick claghen	mixed choir	**W-298**
Serenade	string orch	**W-135**
Quintet 6	cl, vl, vlc, guit, arp	**W-127**
Pastorale	female choir	**W-340**
Ciacona seria (Verses for Fanfare Orchestra)	wind orch	**W-204**

De zoom	female choir	**W-352**
Jubelstadje	female choir	**W-331**

1986

Harpsichord Concerto in A of J. S. Bach	harpsichord and wind orch	**W-235**
Concerto for Trombone	trbn and wind orch	**W-232**
Trio 12	cl, cor ingl, fag	**W-109**
Introduction, Variations and Indonesian Anthem	wind orch	**W-211**
Nachtgesang	female choir	**W-337**
Het lied van Isabella	female choir	**W-329**

1987

Sextet 3	sop, fl, cl, vl, cb, guit	**W-133**
Huygens Suite	chamber orch	**W-138**
Cantata 9 *Christiaan Huygens Cantata*	mixed ch w/orch	**W-246**
O Mistress Mine	mixed choir	**W-291**
Ballade van de omkransde boot	mixed choir	**W-266**
Satire	mixed choir	**W-299**
Tristis est anima mea	mixed choir	**W-301**
Een oudt liedeken	mixed choir	**W-272**
An den Mond	alto, mixed ch	**W-263**
Ave Maris Stella *Hymnus*	mixed choir	**W-264**
Etude (for alternating hands)	carillon	**W-490**
Etude (with arpeggios)	carillon	**W-491**
Pedal Etude	carillon	**W-492**

INDEX

TITLES OF COMPOSITIONS ARE IN *ITALIC* TYPE

About the Author

PAUL KLEMME is assistant professor of music at Washington State University, Pullman, where he conducts the WSU Concert Choir, the Vocal Jazz Ensemble, and teaches conducting, studio voice, and studio organ. He earned the B.Mus. in organ performance from Central Methodist College, the M.Mus. in organ from the University of Michigan, and the D.M.A. in choral conducting from the University of Washington. He has spent the last ten years researching and performing the music of Henk Badings in the United States and Europe.

Gai Rossignol sauvage

Allegretto grazioso

1. Gai rossignol sauvage, Vous qui chantez si bien joyeux refrain, Al-
2. Le rossignol sauvage, Devant qu'il fut parti Plein d'appétit, Pris
3. Le rossignol sauvage, Se pose en arri – vant Et volétant sans

1. – lez faire un mes- sa- ge Dès le ma- tin. Aux pasteurs du vil-
2. son diner d'u- sa- ge D'œuf de fourmi, Mu- ni pour le voy-
3. le plus haut é- ta- ge, Et gazouillant Com- mence son mes-

1. – la ——— ge.
2. a ——— ge.
3. sa ——— ge.

4. Pas- teurs de ce vil- la- ge Je – sus est près de
6. Je vous jure et j'en- gage Pour foi de ce qu'at-

B.f.

p marc.